INSIDE AI  WO

Spiritual experiences of people with autism

Edited by Wolfgang Weirauch

TEMPLE LODGE

Translated from German by Matthew Barton

Temple Lodge Publishing
Hillside House, The Square
Forest Row, RH18 5ES

www.templelodge.com

Published by Temple Lodge 2013

Originally published in German under the title *Autisten berichten* by
Flensburger Hefte Verlag, Flensburg, in 2011

A catalogue record for this book is available from the British Library

ISBN 978 1 906999 51 3

Cover by Morgan Creative incorporating photography
© Creative Studio
Typeset by DP Photosetting, Neath, West Glamorgan
Printed and bound by Gutenberg Press, Malta

Contents

Foreword

This book marks a radical new departure — something which has not happened before in this form. People unable to speak share their thoughts by means of computer-aided communication (called FC or 'Facilitated Communication'). These thoughts do not just describe their current state and immediate experiences but delve far into supersensible realms.

Like all other people in need of special care, and despite constitutional disabilities, those suffering from autism have an ego or I, a core of individuality, that is as intact as anyone else's. It has only relatively recently been discovered that autistic people are just as intelligent as others. Only now though — as reported in this book — can we see that they also have supersensible gifts, can read others' thoughts, communicate with spiritual beings and tell us about their past lives.

As you read further you will come upon unusual and surprising communications, and may feel put off by the strange and special nature of the autistic world. Please stay open-minded: do not dismiss your healthy scepticism but be prepared to be astonished.

The authors of this volume are very unusual but also, nevertheless, quite ordinary people. Though we ourselves are convinced of the authenticity of their supersensible reports, it is important to remember how easy it is to be mistaken in one's spiritual perceptions, and that things essentially true can also sometimes be represented in too one-sided a way — or in a way that does not allow others enough freedom. It is really very difficult to formulate supersensible experience clearly and accurately.

Two autistic brothers and another autistic person speak in these pages to a woman experienced in computer-facilitated communication. Hitherto imprisoned in their bodies, they now give voice to their clairvoyant perceptions. The conversations took place from Christmas 2009 to May 2011 and are presented in chronological order. Since the FC (Facilitated Communication) language is very limited, the style and content of the texts was carefully edited and elaborated—but they largely preserve the original striking and succinct form of language.

What has so far remained hidden is now open for all to see. There is much food for thought here, and we hope you find it both nourishing and stimulating.[*]

Wolfgang Weirauch

---

[*] A detailed interview on autism with care worker Jos Meereboer can be found on p. 169 of this edition.

1 How and Why FC (Facilitated Communication) Works

by Hilke Osika

Hilke Osika, born 1937, grew up near Munich and attended Munich Waldorf School from Class 6 onwards. She dipped into courses in psychology, philosophy, theology and special needs education for a few terms (Munich University, Stuttgart, Eckwälden), then embarked on medical training in Vienna with her husband-to-be. This was interrupted by the birth of a severely disabled child. She had two more healthy children, and then again two equally disabled ones. In 1967 she moved to Sweden. From 1985 she worked at the Vidar Clinic in patient planning and music therapy. In 2005 she trained in FC (Facilitated Communication). Since then she has been a freelance music therapist and an FC partner for various non-speaking people. She also teaches FC.
Contact: *hilke.osika@brevet.nu*

Today there are still countries where parents hide away their child if he or she is born blind. If someone from our culture were to meet such parents and tell them that their child can certainly still learn to read, what would they think of this? Completely blind, and yet still learn to read? Whoever claims this must be mad! Or perhaps he is playing a cruel joke on these parents?

We, by contrast, have accustomed ourselves to the idea that a blind person can read books in Braille script by using the fine touch of his fingertips to feel the diverse arrangements of raised dots on the paper. Helen Keller, who was both blind and deaf, was able to read in several languages, and even speak. She owned a Braille typewriter, allowing her to read what she herself had written, and an ordinary typewriter for texts written for others.

In our civilization, too, it was long thought that deaf children were idiots. They did not reply to questions, did not speak, and seemed not to understand anything. Nowadays we know that this behaviour can conceal a very intelligent individual. If a child is given a chance to learn sign language, he can communicate with others, learn everything possible about the world and express his needs, wishes, thoughts and feelings. He may even learn to lip-read. Helen Keller was able to place her fingers on the lips of the person speaking and by this means 'hear' what he was saying, without seeing the lips.

Thus we have spoken of two senses that may be lacking — those of sight and hearing. And we have seen that ways have been found to help such people, despite such a severe disability, to allow their personality to emerge and express itself.

Yet we have far more senses than these, which can also be impaired. One such is the sense of movement, today called kinaesthesia. This is a less tangible sense for us than vision and hearing. But we can gain insight into it relatively easily by trying the following.

Place your hand on your back and make a fist. Extend the index finger and then the thumb; open the hand and make a fist again. You can't see what you are doing but you feel your movements and can control them.

Now imagine that you were unable to *feel* 'from within' where your hand is positioned and how your fingers move. Imagine your sense of your own movements would not mediate any perception of your hand to your brain. You would have no control over your movements, and could not even make any. You wouldn't even be able to make such movements if you *could* see your hand! Without this mediation by the sense of movement you would have no control over your own movements.

Scores of children and adults suffering from autism are in fact in precisely this situation, especially those unable to speak. If one cannot properly feel the movements of one's hands, it is still possible to use them to push others in order to get something. Perhaps one can pick things up in one's hands and let go of them again. Perhaps, with great effort, one might even carry out more complex hand movements.

It can be still more difficult to master the movements of one's mouth. If we cannot inwardly sense where our lips, tongue and lower jaw are and how they move, it will be very arduous indeed, or even impossible, to learn to speak. Some people in this situation can scarcely learn to chew.

The worst thing of all is probably being unable to feel the movements of facial muscles and control them. Such a person cannot show that he understands what others say! He cannot even show interest, and then everyone around him will think it's not worth telling him anything. It may be assumed that he has a very low IQ.

And yet a fully intelligent and skilled person can be locked in the dungeon of this functionally impaired body. We shy away from thinking about this—it seems inconceivable and appalling. The idea this might be so is almost unbearable.

Some mothers have intuitively placed their hands around those of their autistic child, using the child's hands to do things in this way: to pick something up from the ground, to eat with spoon or fork, to put on socks, etc. This has proven helpful. By feeling the touch of the mother's hands around their own hands, these children can better sense their own hands, even if only from without, through the sense of touch. When someone else touches them this can also help to overcome possible psychomotor dysfunction.

Some people with autism cannot point to anything, not even with their whole hand. They will stand in front of all the cakes and buns in a café without being able to indicate the cake they are longing for. Instead they will just look at you expectantly or push your arm in a vague direction. But if you place your hand on theirs, and ask again, it is possible they will be able to point to the cake.

This is how FC (Facilitated Communication) works. Here, the person with autism (let's call him A) receives the help necessary for *feeling* his hand and so being able to *point* to something — no longer in a rough direction but exactly to the intended point.

The person who helps A takes hold of A's right hand with her right hand from below, with a certain degree of upward pressure, forming it so that A's index finger is pointing forwards. With her left hand the supporter uses her index finger and thumb to touch A's elbow or, to put it more precisely, the two protruding joint bones of the elbow. This serves as tactile stimulus. A needs to *feel* this joint, albeit from without through another person. The elbow joint is in fact the only joint that needs to be moved when pointing. (If A is left-handed, the helper adapts this support accordingly.)

Careful research has been done to work out how best to develop collaboration between the helper and A. Emotional support is also important, as is explaining to A at the beginning what is involved in the whole process. This evolves from pointing to photographs and identifying known people, through pointing to pictures with various already listed alternative answers (e.g. 'yes' or 'no'), to pointing to letters, letters on a letter chart, or later to letters on the computer keyboard.

Frequently, to everyone's astonishment, A already knows the letters and can even spell to some extent. This can be explained as follows. People with autism are usually very gifted visually. It is much harder for them to identify individual words and their meaning amidst the plethora of words they hear. In place of the countless nuances of spoken language, written language consists of just 26 letters in varying combinations. And these written words stay where they are — one can return to them time and again to better understand them, in contrast to uttered words. The child sees written script everywhere, on packaging, adverts, etc.

FC does not seek to replace sign language, pictures or other communication aids. One of its advantages, however, is that one can retain one's usual language and ordinary script.

However, learning FC is not straightforward. On the one hand one has to learn to avoid any manipulation — that is, somehow leading A's finger to a letter one is thinking of oneself. And on the other, one must learn to follow A's intentions with great sensitivity. This requires training and thorough practice, along with guidance from an experienced facilitator, before one may work with someone with autism. And then too one needs both ongoing training and supervision. Additionally one needs to train in gradually relinquishing facilitation. (Some severely autistic people can now write quite independently, without any support — but this takes years of conscious practice.)

FC usually does not work if an untrained person tries to write with A, even if A is already used to writing on the computer. This is because it is very easy for FC users to become insecure or unsettled.

Training includes learning how to arrange material that A will point to, the starting position to return to after every pointing action or typing of a letter, and the degree of resistance needed for A to carry out his pointing actions in a more targeted way. Adapting this resistance to an often fluctuating muscle tone and to A's needs without interfering in or halting the process can be very demanding.

With young children who have difficulty identifying letters/speech sounds, one first practises pointing as such — to items of food, and pictures. One then introduces them to written language by writing out possible choices and getting them to indicate what they wish with the help of a letter chart. If one starts this in good time, some of these non-speaking children can be integrated into normal primary schooling with a support person who will also need other special needs skills.

If A is already adult when FC begins, however, nothing but real communication is involved. One does not ask A anything to which one already knows the answer. One would not do this to any other competent person. With love and genuine interest we ask A things we really wish to know, or ask about matters we think might interest him and which we ourselves wish to engage with. And we also tell A about ourselves, just as in any other friendly communication. Thus the situation is never one of interrogation.

Quite often an FC conversation will start with us asking what A himself would like to tell or ask us.

Traditional communication systems generally use a selection of ready-made images, signs and similar, so that one cannot really express anything unique to oneself. It is therefore a further advantage of FC that A can relate things that no one has ever previously thought of. This is only possible of course if A has mastered written language.

Many FC users never previously showed any interest in learning to read and write, and their lack of interest was ascribed to defective cognitive skills. But now, with the prospect of communicating things personal to them, they learn very quickly — supported by our immediate utterance of each indicated or typed letter — to arrange letters in the right sequence so that we can understand the word they are thinking of. To begin with their independent deletion of wrongly chosen letters is very important here. Written language thus soon becomes an extremely good and flexible way of expressing their own wishes, feelings and points of view.

When working on the computer we can take it in turns to write, giving rise to real conversations. While A writes, we clearly speak each letter and each word aloud. We also do this, at least at the beginning, when we write our own half of the conversation as facilitator. After our own or A's portion of the dialogue, we read the whole section aloud again before writing further. This helps A to understand, and may even help him to start speaking. A sees the written words and at the same time hears them being spoken very clearly.

Some people with autism who cannot speak, think in a different way from us. This likewise requires our training and supervision if we wish to work with FC.

Autism can manifest in very different ways. Some people with 'high-functioning autism' have described how their senses leave them in the lurch. Certain senses do not function normally, especially their perception of their own body and its functions.[*]

Almost all those with autism and Asperger's have in common a certain clumsiness and difficulty in smoothly coordinating their movements. Do those who cannot speak just suffer from a more severe form of this sensory disorder?

A young, non-speaking, very autistic Swedish man recently wrote after five months of FC: 'It is claustrophobic not to be able to express one's feelings and thoughts; not to be able to clearly express what one wishes to say, one's

---

[*] See for example Donna Williams, *Somewhere*, Jessica Kingsley Publishers, 1998, and works by Dietmar Zöller, Temple Grandin, Susanne Schäfer and others.

needs and wishes.' And he also wrote how important FC had now become for him.

FC has been used for the past 20 years now, in several countries and by hundreds of people with disability. If we consider that for several decades of the last century, in certain countries, deaf children were not allowed to learn sign language because people wanted them to learn to lip-read exclusively, we can ask how long autistic people will be forced to wait without any access to language before we allow them to participate in life in a more equal way.

The means used to communicate with blind or deaf people are now commonplace. In a very similar way, experiences with FC represent a challenge and a respon-sibility to develop real communication with autistic people whose capacity for speech is either limited or wholly lacking.

2 How Can One Help Children with Autism?

Hilke and Erik Osika

Erik Osika, born 1970, has lived in good therapeutic homes since he was 8. He was not allowed to attend normal schools, which was a cause of great suffering for him. Erik sees poorly and walks with difficulty. He can feed himself and throw things away! He has compulsive behaviour and often grinds his teeth loudly and involuntarily. With the aid of FC he reports that he does not feel his body, and therefore cannot control it. He is wonderful to converse and consult with (through FC). He mostly has humorous, bantering conversations with staff at his home.

Erik is a fairly short man, and my beloved son for the past 40 years. He did not arrive on earth alone but with his twin brother Markus. Both have severe autism and cannot speak a word. Erik's gait is somewhat idiosyncratic and he is unable to do anything with his hands except eat with knife and fork and dress or undress himself—with help. He can move things around or put them in the waste bin—where often one finds biros, cups, dish brushes and other 'unnecessary things'. His right eye tends to be swollen because he hits it with his fist when he's sad or feels misunderstood. But it was much worse five years ago. Until then we all thought that he didn't understand anything.

Since I have three children with this severe form of autism (as well as two healthy children), I read a great deal about autism, attended lectures and courses on it, and ultimately gave lectures and courses myself. In the process, of course, I had heard about Facilitated Communication—a method which Rosemarie Crossley developed in Australia in the 80s. But my own children, I thought, were far too disabled for such a method.

But then, five years ago, I got hold of the DVD of the Swiss film 'My Thinking Language'.[*] I wanted to show this to my two normal children, but my son, a doctor, refused to even watch it but told me, with a physician's authority, that I should go to Switzerland and learn this communication method. He had already said, previously, that this was something one should try out with his beloved brothers.

So I contacted Bea Kaufmann in Zurich, who had been working with autism for 40 years and had taught FC for the past ten years. She visited us in Sweden, partly on vacation but also to meet my sons and teach me FC. She demonstrated how FC works to my three sons and two other non-speaking adults, and all five showed within two hours that they knew the letters and could reply to her questions in simple words.

I thought I was dreaming. This couldn't be possible! But I cancelled my planned trip to Iceland and instead drove each day to the institution where these men with autism live. After ten days I progressed from writing on the alphabet board to the laptop keyboard, because I wanted to save and document the interesting things that these men wrote.

It took a few weeks for me to really grasp the reality of this, and why and how it works. It soon becomes apparent however that people with autism do not relate to 'facts' in the same down-to-earth way as we do, and that they do not always experience reality like us—but are more interested in music, serious discussions and spiritual matters. When we communicate with them with the aid of a computer, they become more familiar with our daily reality and we enter their interesting world of thoughts and experiences—as long as we are open and unprejudiced enough.

---

[*] *Meine Denksprache*, not available in English.

First conversation:

Hilke: There is a young woman training to be a curative teacher whose final dissertation is about how to help children with autism. She asked me, but I can only say something about FC and also about children with Asperger's. You have written that you would like to suggest how one can help children with autism, and you're an expert in this field! How can one help children with autism?

Erik: One can do a great deal by giving them love.

Hilke: How can one show them love?

Erik: One can embrace them.

Hilke: Should one embrace them even if they resist this?

Erik: Then one shouldn't embrace them, but kiss them instead.

Hilke: When they are children with Asperger's, one is meant to always treat them as if they are much older and more sensible than their actual age suggests. How is this for children with autism?

Erik: They also want to be treated with dignity, as though they are much older and more reasonable than they seem to be.

Hilke: So do they understand what one says to them?

Erik: It varies, and it depends on what you say and whether you really visualize what you're speaking about.

Hilke: So you should really picture what you're thinking while you speak, and that will help?

Erik: Yes.

Hilke: Someone recently told me that it helped autistic children to get dressed if she pictured to herself how they would put on the next item of clothing. Is that right?

Erik: Yes, that's right.

Hilke: I myself have found that children can learn to do things with their hands when I put my hands on theirs and guide them.

Erik: That's the best way to do it.

Hilke: I got the sense that these children are not very interested in practical things like money, or how much something costs. What are they interested in?

Erik: They are interested in what people around them are interested in.

Hilke: What might that be?

Erik: It could be religion, music, science. Or God, or books about art history or very interesting hobbies like plant breeding or feeding animals that can't survive over winter.

Hilke: How can one communicate one's interests and hobbies to such children?

Erik: You can take them with you and tell them about your own interests. But if they show no interest, these things are still important to them! It does not mean they are not interested.

Hilke: What about art and art museums?

Erik: They are always interested in art.

Hilke: Parents have found that autistic children don't appear to look at paintings in galleries.

Erik: They see everything with one glance, and then they can live into the artwork's aura.

Hilke: It can be more difficult with concerts because these children can make so much noise they disturb others, and parents can't cope with it.

Erik: Parents could go to church concerts and sit in the back row. Then they can take their child out if he's disruptive.

Hilke: Yes, sometimes we did that. It helped one child for me to massage his feet when he got too enthusiastically vocal.

Erik: It is good for all of them to receive massage or chirophonetics.

Hilke: Should the massage be on their legs, back or somewhere else?

Erik: On their legs and feet.

Hilke: I have heard one should massage their legs with a thick towel that is not too soft.

Erik: I am sure that would be good.

Hilke: Is there anything in particular that children should be given to eat, or anything they ought not to eat?

Erik: I can't comment on that.

Hilke: There are autistic children who bite, scratch or hit themselves. They can do themselves real harm.

Erik: They have no other way of expressing themselves, and are desperate.

Hilke: What should one do?

Erik: One can help them with FC. That's the best thing of all for them.

Hilke: Yes, certainly it is. I also have the feeling that one reinforces this self-harming by trying to stop them, and by getting worked up and desperate oneself.

Erik: That's true, for then [if you don't get worked up] they understand that someone cares about their behaviour.

Hilke: And we want them to know that, but wish to avoid them harming themselves. Apart from FC, what else can one do here?

Erik: They do it because they can't feel it hurting. They need a response, but not one that harms them.

Hilke: When they hurt themselves, or get in a terrible rage, we can feel very desperate, afraid or angry. If, on the other hand, they do something positive and good, we have positive feelings but not nearly such strong ones.

Erik: Then they will repeat these terrible ways of behaving instead of the positive ones.

Hilke: Is there some way for us to strengthen our positive responses so that these become as attractive as our despairing ones?

Erik: You yourself can control your reactions so well that you scarcely react to unfortunate behaviour, but respond strongly to good kinds.

Hilke: And that's good?

Erik: Of course!

Hilke: I try at least never to make too much of a fuss but to respond with real feelings—which perhaps I allow to emerge.

Erik: That's why we can experience your reaction as desirable.

Hilke: I am very pleased! What other things should one consider when looking after children with severe autism?

Erik: We can't understand how you know so much but do not know what we are thinking.

Hilke: Sometimes I had the sense that you [plural] think we can read others' thoughts like you can—that you think of something you want to have or want to do, but that we are so mean to you that we just go ahead and do something different which you didn't want or which you hadn't thought of. Reading others' thoughts is something we'll have to learn in future, but before then we'll need to acquire loving selflessness. You've got further with that than we have. Then we'll see that we shouldn't exploit this skill egotistically, but only in order to help others.

Erik: That's really important.

Hilke: I'd like to ask you something else now. Every week you went to the Vidar Clinic to have music therapy, and at that time we weren't yet able to communicate with each other. Each time we went to the café I tried to teach you to choose a piece of cake, and show me which one you wanted. But you just glanced quickly at the cakes and then looked back at me expectantly.

Erik: Back then I didn't know that you couldn't read my thoughts. I thought you would give me the cake I was thinking of. But you gave me a different one, and I was disappointed.

Hilke: And I didn't know you were unable to point unless I press your hand or your arm. Are you able to point to the cake you'd like now, with my support?

Erik: You know I can.

Hilke: Do you have further advice or any tip for us ordinary people?

Erik: That you go to a good person and learn from him.

Hilke: Whenever I have told people with autism that unfortunately I'm not able to read their thoughts, they have looked at me without any understanding and gone on gazing at me expectantly. They seem not to believe it.

Erik: Hilke can sometimes read thoughts, but she is unaware of this. It becomes clearer when we write.

Hilke: Then perhaps I am on the right path?

Erik: Yes, but the others still have to learn it by not thinking themselves while they support us.

Hilke: It's particularly important for us not to think ourselves while supporting you in FC, so that you can really express what you wish to say without our thoughts disturbing or influencing you.

Erik: That's not easy, but you are good at it.

Hilke: That is very important for me and really not so easy ... Should children with severe autism attend ordinary schools, and simply sit there alongside the other children? Or would it be better for them to attend special schools and learn certain things there?

Erik: I don't know any special schools.

Hilke: That's true. On the Continent, some children with autism who can't speak attend ordinary schools and have an FC facilitator to support them. Then they can take part in lessons, but have to write down all their replies and their essays using FC.

Erik: I would really have liked that; but you all thought that I couldn't understand anything.

Hilke: Sadly that's absolutely true. I only learned FC five years ago. When proprioception, perception of one's own movements in space, kinaesthesia, do not function, one cannot feel one's own muscles moving, and then it's impossible to control them. Then one can neither speak nor use facial expression or gestures to express oneself. But when you were still a child, FC had not yet been developed. Let us hope that in future children with autism will have the good fortune to be able to communicate in this way.

Erik: Yes, let us really hope this happens.

Second conversation

Hilke: Erik, now we can continue our conversation. This morning after breakfast you did something which might help us better understand autism. You threw lots of pretzels in the rubbish bin. Before that you had thrown wet dish brushes in, and this made the pretzels wet and inedible. I said to you that we could have eaten the pretzels later, when we were hungry again, and you replied that you hadn't thought of that. Is it hard for children with autism to plan for the future? How do they experience time?

Erik: They can't think of the future.

Hilke: What time do they think of?

Erik: Only the one that is present now.

Hilke: Are they unable to think of the future or don't they want to, or are they afraid of the future?

Erik: They can't think of the future.

Hilke: Is there any way to teach them to think of the future and learn to plan?

Erik: I know of none.

Hilke: There is a method for doing this, called TEACHH. For example, you hang up a board in the hallway where everyone often passes, and place pictures there showing everything that's meant to happen during the day, and the sequence. In this way children can get a sense of what will happen later on. You've never tried this, but what is your view of it?

Erik: That sounds good. I'd like to try it.

Hilke: Do you think that your friends where you live would be interested in this?

Erik: I'm sure they would.

Hilke: How is it with things that have already happened? How do children with autism remember things?

Erik: They remember everything they have experienced. They continually think of it.

Hilke: Do they think more about what they have experienced in the past than about what is happening right now?

Erik: That question is too hard.

Hilke: Do they usually have happy or worrying memories, and can they themselves choose what they want to remember?

Erik: They can't choose what they remember, but the words they hear trigger memories.

Hilke: An adult with autism said that he sees everything connected with a memory passing before him as in a film, and that he cannot just focus on one detail. Is this true for others with autism?

Erik: That's true of everyone with autism.

Hilke: So is it true that we others are the ones who cause pleasant or painful memories depending on what we say to a child with autism?

Erik: I always preferred to hear pleasing words with pleasant memories.

Hilke: Would you give me some examples?

Erik: Perhaps words that reminded me of my birthday.

Hilke: For us others it can be difficult to be completely sure which memories may have been pleasant for such children, since they can't control their facial expressions, and so we can't always tell whether an experience has made them happy, anxious or disappointed.

Erik: I can understand that.

Hilke: Have you any advice about what we could do or say to ensure a child has pleasant memories?

Erik: You just have to keep on trying until you manage it. You can see whether the child wants to speak to you by whether he looks into your eyes. Then the child is trying to tell you that he wants to hear more.

Hilke: I didn't know this. If a child is happy that one is talking about a pleasant birthday experience, can one then talk about it again repeatedly? We ordinary folk would soon get bored if we had to keep listening to the same thing. How is this for children with autism?

Erik: They can listen to the same thing many times, without getting bored. On the contrary, each time it is just as pleasing again as before.

Hilke: In fact we cannot converse with children who never reply and never show in any other way that they understand anything of what we are saying.

Erik: That's a shame, since they'd like to know everything that you can tell them. You told us about fine, wise things which taught us a lot.

Hilke: How nice to hear this—I don't remember. For instance, I never told any stories from my own childhood until we were able to write with FC, and you showed that you were interested. Should one read fairy tales to these children?

Erik: Yes, that's good, and everything else that is appropriate for children.

Hilke: Can one just go on talking, or do they get tired of listening?

Erik: They don't get tired at all.

Hilke: But what if they are jumping about and running off, and don't show the least interest?

Erik: It doesn't matter, they are still listening.

Hilke: Another strange thing is what they do with their hands. We use our hands to do things we think are useful or necessary. It is very difficult for children with autism to learn this. Instead, they do things with their hands that often disturb or irritate us.

Erik: They can't feel their hands, but their hands do things they can't control. They don't want this to happen but they observe it and find it interesting.

Hilke: But what is actually governing their hands?

Erik: Subconscious drives and cravings.

Hilke: I would never have thought of this. Then I also understand why it is so terrible to just tell them off for doing what seems crazy, and that this could have the opposite effect. It must be terrible to be reproached for what one cannot consciously control.

Erik: Yes, it's really terrible! You can't imagine how terrible this is.

Hilke: Yes, the children can't tell us, and we have no idea that this is so. Many children with autism find it hard to look into our eyes. Do you know why?

Erik: It's because they can't endure the other's gaze, because it is too strong.

Hilke: Can you explain that more?

Erik: They feel exposed. For a long time, without anyone knowing this, I've been helped by seeing so badly that I can cope with people's gaze.

Hilke: What is the effect of our gaze on these children?

Erik: It torments them because they don't know what it means.

Hilke: Someone wrote that when we try to look into such a child's eyes, and speak and move at the same time, this causes too many sensory impressions. Is that right?

Erik: That is possible with some children.

Hilke: Those who use the Son-Rise method with autistic people believe that it is good for the child to get used to eye contact. For instance they say one can hold a picture book in front of one so that the child sees the pictures directly below the adult's eyes. The adult tells the story and tries to catch the child's gaze. What do you think about this?

Erik: It seems good, for then the child can understand what the adult wants.

Hilke: Don't they know otherwise what we adults would like them to do?

Erik: They never otherwise understand what you adults want them to do.

Hilke: Even when we tell them what we want?

Erik: No, they don't understand commands because they are unable to carry out what is expected of them.

Hilke: How could we improve this? Do you have an idea?

Erik: One could ask them to do something, then help them to do it, and repeat this every day.

Hilke: That's sounds sensible, and I hadn't thought of it.

Third conversation

Hilke: Dear Erik, now I'd like to ask you about music. What kind of music are autistic children interested in do you think?

Erik: Classical music, above all Mozart.

Hilke: Why?

Erik: It's Christian music.

Hilke: Does it matter if the music you listen to is live music, or on the radio or a CD?

Erik: Chinese music is good too.

Hilke: Typical Chinese music is mostly pentatonic: five tones per octave without semitones in between.

Erik: Yes, that's the kind.

Hilke: Are there instruments which autistic children could play themselves?

Erik: Lyre and glockenspiel

Hilke: Do you mean the kind that are tuned pentatonically, made by Auris?

Erik: Yes, the children can play those themselves.

Hilke: I have found that autistic children cannot touch the lyre strings themselves but prefer to strike them with a small drumstick.

Erik: I can understand that. It is unpleasant to stroke the lyre with your fingers because the strings are so hard.

Hilke: You did not answer when I asked about live or recorded music.

Erik: Live music is best, but recorded is also good.

Hilke: How about painting?

Erik: It would be good to paint using FC.

Hilke: Do you mean that one could put pressure on the child's hand as he holds the brush or the crayon, so that he feels his hand and can then use it to point to the colour he wants to use, or so that the child can guide his hand to create the forms he wishes to draw?

Erik: That's what I mean.

Hilke: But it isn't easy to keep pressing the child's hand and at the same time staying very sensitive to his artistic impulses relating to colours and forms on the paper — in other words both to press his hand and at the same time completely relinquish any effort at 'assisting' him, just following his impulses and not affecting them.

Erik: I understand, but you'd be welcome to learn this! I would recommend it!

Hilke: What about modelling?

Erik: It would be good for them to try this out; preferably with colours.

Hilke: Any other art form?

Erik: I don't know.

Hilke: Do children with autism have religious needs?

Erik: They like you to say an evening prayer with them. They like accompanying you to church.

Hilke: Many children with autism have poor eyesight, but they pick up tiny things from the ground in front of them.

Erik: They do that because they love tiny little things.

Hilke: But then they throw them away again just as quickly!

Erik: It is fun to throw things away. But these little things draw their attention because they are so small and fine.

Hilke: Why do these children love such small, fine things?

Erik: Because things of normal size are too hard for them to handle.

Hilke: That makes sense. Could one use this preference of theirs for a good purpose or to nurture their development?

Erik: Maybe they could pick up small beads from the ground and place them in a bowl.

Hilke: That seems like a good idea. Would that be like a game which involves pouring the beads out on the ground again so as to pick them up once more?

Erik: No, not straight away. Maybe the next day again.

Hilke: How about jigsaw puzzles?

Erik: It would be good if they could learn this.

Hilke: Would the picture itself be important, or would the shapes of the puzzle pieces be more important do you think?

Erik: Probably the shapes when you put the puzzle together.

Hilke: Is there anything else these children should try?

Erik: Having a pet.

Hilke: Are you thinking of any particular kind of pet, or would you recommend one?

Erik: Golden hamsters in a hutch.

Hilke: I didn't know you'd heard of these animals! Is there any special reason for this type of hamster?

Erik: Because they aren't so sensitive but they're fun.

Hilke: Should the children learn to look after these animals themselves, or is that asking too much?

Erik: The children can be present when the animal is fed, and can feed it themselves.

Hilke: Another thing which children with autism seem to love is to rock their body back and forth.

Erik: It's a nice feeling, rocking like that. It helps you feel your body better.

Hilke: And some of these children like waggling their hands in various ways. Why do they do this?

Erik: It's also so that they can feel their body better.

Hilke: We always have a sense of our body and are aware of where its boundaries lie. We know where our hands and legs are, and how they move. How is this for children with autism?

Erik: It is quite different for them. They can't feel their body's boundaries, nor where their arms and legs are or how these move.

Hilke: How troublesome that must be!

Erik: It isn't troublesome at all but lovely.

Hilke: But still lovelier when one feels one's body by rocking or waggling one's hands?

Erik: Yes.

Hilke: Not feeling one's body causes problems. One is unable to use the body to speak as one would like, nor the hands to do with them what one wants. You mentioned that massage might improve this. Is there anything else you can advise? Or is it fine not to do so much with your hands and not to be able to speak?

Erik: It isn't at all good not to speak and not to be able to use one's hands better! But we will be able to do this in our next life.

Hilke: It sounds as if this thought could be very comforting. Are there children who think this way?

Erik: All children with autism think like that.

Hilke: May I ask how they come upon such a thought?

Erik: Their angel tells them this before they are born.

Hilke: And they remember it?

Erik: Yes, and they hear it every night.

Hilke: But is there any point at all then in trying to help such children develop towards doing what normal children can do?

Erik: It's far more important than you realize — for then we can start at a higher level in our next life.

Hilke: What more might we do to help these children feel their body better, apart from massage and chirophonetics. Is there anything else?

Erik: FC.

Hilke: Yes, FC is a blessing, and without it we wouldn't even have been able to have this conversation. Should we go on considering how one can help children with autism?

Erik: We can go on with it another time.

Fourth conversation

Hilke: Dear Erik, now you have written on the alphabet board that you want us to continue our conversation. Did you think of another way of helping children with autism?
Erik: You have no idea how important our discussion might be for children with autism.
Hilke: Yes, it's an important discussion. But if it is going to help these children, then many who support autistic children need to read it and take part in it. And I'm not talking about autistic children who can speak. How should I do this?
Erik: You can send it to interested people who can distribute it.
Hilke: Do you know any?
Erik: No, you must find them yourself.
Hilke: I'll try. Do you have other suggestions about how one could help children with autism?
Erik: You must ask me.
Hilke: Gladly! Many children with autism sniff around at things and people, their hair and arms, etc.
Erik: Many other children do this too.
Hilke: That's true, but others tend not to do it so much and so intently, and they stop much sooner. Why do they want to smell everything?
Erik: They smell everything because this tells them things about people.
Hilke: What kind of things does it tell them?
Erik: Whether it's a good person or someone with bad intentions, or whether the person is 'junketing' with another.
Hilke: It's said that dogs can smell whether people are afraid. What does it mean if they are 'junketing' with someone?
Erik: It means trying to hoodwink them.
Hilke: That sounds as if one can detect many different smells on people. Is that so?

Erik: Yes. There are an enormous number of smells.

Hilke: Then these children have a much better, clearer sense of smell than we others! They may have further developed the ordinary sense of smell of young children because they can't learn so many other things. Might this be so? Or is this excellent sense of smell a natural gift?

Erik: Both things are true. They are very interested in all kinds of smell.

On the last evening of our conversation I was absolutely exhausted. Erik smelled the back of my head, as he has been doing recently, and when I asked him how it smelled he replied, 'catastrophic'. I asked him why it smelled like that and he said, 'because you are so tired.' The next day my head smelled 'good', although I hadn't washed my hair.

Hilke: Can we do something to give pleasure to these children through smells, or nurture their development in some way by using smells?

Erik: That's a hard question.

Hilke: Do these children like it when we wear perfume?

Erik: They don't like perfume.

Hilke: I wonder whether we should use scented or unscented washing powder. When one washes clothes with unscented washing powder, they don't smell so good to us. I myself use expensive washing powder with natural lemon grass fragrance. What do you think about that.

Erik: It's best without perfume.

Hilke: Do you experience the smell of lemon grass as a perfume?

Erik: No.

Hilke: What smells do these children like?

Erik: Quite a few, such as 'oranga', opium, and also powdered herbs such as cinnamon and vanilla.

Hilke: Interesting! Unfortunately I don't know what 'oranga' is.

Erik: They are oranges.

Hilke: And opium is meant to be contained in some perfumes. Did you mean that?

Erik: No, I meant the counter-grounds for junior ginger.

Hilke: Now I understand still less! Did you mean the smell when someone uses opium as a narcotic?

Erik: That's the kind of thing I meant.

Hilke: If smoking opium creates a desirable smell, I hope nevertheless that not too many children are exposed to it!

Erik: I can understand that!

Hilke: Yesterday we passed a flower shop and I asked myself whether children with autism might enjoy all the flower scents.

Erik: I believe some of them would.

Hilke: If these children usually have such a strongly developed sense of smell, I wonder what their sense of taste is like, since they so much like putting salt and sugar on their food. Are natural tastes not something they experience?

Erik: Food tastes boring.

Hilke: They can distinguish many different smells. Can they distinguish a great many different nuances of taste in the same way?

Erik: No.

Hilke: Can we do anything about this? Too much salt or sugar is harmful to health. Do you have an idea?

Erik: You could spice food with herbs, for instance with a tiny bit of pepper; also paprika or curry powder. I myself prefer marjoram and thyme.

Hilke: Some of these children seem to find it difficult to recognize people they know in different surroundings from the usual ones. What is this due to?

Erik: I always recognized people.

Hilke: Do you mind if I ask a silly question? How did you recognize people — by their face, their smell, or something else?

Erik: I recognize them through their aura and their different personalities.

Hilke: Children with Asperger's syndrome find it very difficult indeed to understand others' thoughts and feelings. They can't empathize with how others feel. How is this for children with autism who can't speak?

Erik: They feel very strongly what others feel and think.

Hilke: Does this go directly into them or can they defend themselves against it, and maintain their own feelings and thoughts?

Erik: It goes directly into them and they are completely overwhelmed by it but can't show this.

Hilke: What should we try to do when we are near them?

Erik: You should only feel and think what it would be right for the child to hear if you said it aloud.

Hilke: So we must learn something in relation to autistic children that is no doubt as difficult for us to learn as some things we try to teach them! And to learn to control our thoughts and feelings ourselves is no doubt good for us?

Erik: Yes, it's good for your development.

Hilke: Autistic children seem to have a good sense of hearing — or perhaps over-sensitive, since they put their hands over their ears sometimes or get in a rage when they hear high or harsh noises; even noises we usually hardly notice, like an air conditioner or a baby crying far away.

Erik: That's really true. You have no idea how troublesome all loud noises are!

Hilke: How can we help these children?

Erik: One could speak more quietly, and take them away from loud noises.

Hilke: Another thing is trying to hear individual words from the stream of words when someone speaks. What is this like?

Erik: It's very difficult, almost impossible.

Hilke: What can we do to make this possible?

Erik: You can just say single words when you want us to understand what you want us to do.

Hilke: But if we write on the computer as we are doing now, then you can read what I've just written. What's happening here?

Erik: That's quite different. I can read each word myself, and can understand every word.

Hilke: It is striking that many children and adults with autism can't read script on the computer screen unless one enlarges it. Often it has to be 36 point instead of 10 or 12 point, which we usually use. This must mean that most people with autism are short-sighted without us knowing, and that they therefore cannot read ordinary books.

Erik: That is true. I can't read ordinary books, but I can read large-print books.

Hilke: Some children who are prescribed glasses after an eye test, keep pulling them off.

Erik: They want to wear them so they can read, but their hands can't get used to the glasses.

Hilke: Does this feel unpleasant on their face?

Erik: Yes, it feels odd.

Hilke: Can we help here?

Erik: Their hands would have to learn to tolerate the glasses.

Hilke: Someone asked me to tie his hands so that he wouldn't keep pulling his glasses off. But I don't want to do that.

Erik: One could tie his hands up every day until the child has got used to the glasses.

Hilke: Thanks for the tip! Then there are autistic children who keep taking their clothes off however cold or hot it is. Other children never want to get undressed. What is their sense of warmth like?

Erik: They don't feel how warm it is.

Hilke: Don't they feel cold sometimes?

Erik: No.

Hilke: But surely there are other children whose sense of warmth does function well?

Erik: There may be.

Hilke: Then we also have a sense of touch, as well as the so-called 'stroking sense' for very light touch on the body. What is the sense of touch like, do you think, in children with autism?

Erik: The sense of touch is often very poorly developed. This sense does not convey touch but instead pain.

Hilke: What sort of pain?

Erik: It hurts them when you embrace them. But it doesn't hurt to be embraced well, in a very gentle way.

Hilke: I am sure that is true for some children, but others prefer strong embraces, and if one touches or embraces them too lightly this hurts them.

Erik: That's not so in my case.

Hilke: But some autistic children seem scarcely to feel things that hurt normal children, for instance when they burn themselves, get their hand stuck in a door or some other kind of injury. You yourself told me that they do not feel it when they bite or hit themselves.

Erik: I've also noticed that.

Hilke: There is another sense that tells us whether we need to go to the toilet, for either a pee or a poo, whether we are hungry, thirsty or full, whether we are tired or feeling ill. In other words, things going on inside the body. How is this for children with autism?

Erik: This sense functions poorly. I don't always know when I need a pee.

Hilke: Is there anything we can do to help improve this?

Erik: Yes, it can get a good deal better if people keep telling me I should go to the loo.

Hilke: Another thing we clearly should not tell children off for?

Erik: When they have an 'accident' they cannot understand it themselves. And nor do they understand why they are getting told off.

Hilke: And what about eating and drinking? There are children who eat and drink too much or too little, or only very particular things.

Erik: They never feel full.

Hilke: What can one do for such children?

Erik: I don't know.

Hilke: I wondered whether some of these children have an over-sensitive mouth. Some only like puréed food, and refuse to try anything else. They may be afraid that the food might scratch their mouth.

Erik: It might be so, I don't know.

Hilke: Sometimes it seemed to me that autistic children can have terrible outbursts but hardly remember them afterwards. Is that possible?

Erik: It's possible if they themselves don't notice that they have terrible feelings. Then they can't remember this afterwards either.

Hilke: Can one help them to become more aware of their feelings?

Erik: One can say to them: Now you are angry, or now you feel despair.

Hilke: Then they can gradually learn to recognize their own feelings?

Erik: Yes, and this helps them to control them. This is true of normal children as well.

Hilke: Dad had a question about craftwork for older children. He thinks that crafts are important for people with autism. But it isn't easy to find a craft that people with severe autism can learn and practise. Is there any particular kind of craft you recommend?

Erik: No, I don't think that craft is the right occupation for people with autism. They should do something else, such as eurythmy with FC, listening to music and writing with FC, and learning to play an instrument.

Hilke: As to writing with FC, could they write anything other than conversations?

Erik: Yes, they could write books and novels.

Hilke: What could the books be about?

Erik: They could be about history, they could be about medieval times and the Hitler period.

Hilke: Would you like to write a book of that kind?

Erik: I would like to, but first I would have to learn more about these periods.

Hilke: I will see whether we can get hold of large-print books about these periods. May I ask whether you yourself can turn the pages of a book?

Erik: No, I can't. You'll have to help me.

Hilke: We could train this skill together perhaps, with my hands on yours. There are also audiobooks, books spoken on CDs. What would you think of listening to a book of that kind about history?

Erik: We can try it, but it will be hard for me to understand what is being said.

Hilke: An audiobook like that can be heard again and again.

Erik: That would be a good idea.

Hilke: What other way could you imagine for finding out more about historical events?

Erik: If J. would give a lecture on it.

Hilke: He gives wonderful, interesting lectures. Can you get the words out of the word stream when he does? Do you understand what he is talking about?

Erik: I do understand, because all the time he is speaking you are thinking what he says.

Hilke: If he isn't planning to give a lecture on these periods of history, would it be possible for you to understand me if I were to read a book about it?

Erik: This would be possible if I were in the same room. You could read quietly. But every word you read you would have to think as well.

Hilke: If I found a book in German or English and read it while you were in the room, would that work?

Erik: You would have to think it in Swedish.

Hilke: That would be possible. Tell me, how long have you been able to read my thoughts so clearly?

Erik: I have always been able to do this.

Hilke: Can you read other people's thoughts as clearly?

Erik: I can with W. and I., but not so well with the others. It works better with you [plural] because you think so clearly.

Hilke: Do the others think more in feelings, or how do they think?

Erik: They don't think such clear thoughts, but you [plural] think in whole sentences.

Hilke: So this might be another thing to practise if one wants to engage with autistic children?

Erik: Yes, anyone who has anything to do with us and who wants us to understand them should learn this.

Hilke: Is there anything else we ought to learn?

Erik: To meditate, for then we can understand each other better.

Hilke: Why would we understand each other better?

Erik: Because we meditate every day — the children do too.

Hilke: What do you meditate on?

Erik: The children meditate on inner experiences and we adults on the mantras we have received from our spiritual teachers.

Hilke: So you are engaging in self-development, but in a different realm from us?

Erik: Yes, we may be doing this precisely because we are disabled.

Hilke: How does one meditate?

Erik: It is important to sit down calmly and quietly, and think of a wise person's saying. Then one refrains from rushing on to another thought but instead dwells in this thought for as long as one can concentrate on the saying or verse. You have to feel the words in your heart too. It is good if one can meditate every day. Five minutes are enough for beginners. It isn't good that I'm writing this, for it is easily misunderstood.

Hilke: How can this be understood?

Erik: Because people might think we autistic people are mystics of some kind. But that's not right.

Fifth conversation

Hilke: Erik, you've written on the alphabet board that you'd like to continue our conversation. Is there anything in particular we should discuss?

Erik: Yes, we should talk about why we can't communicate with everyone.

Hilke: An interesting and important question. Why can't you?

Erik: Hilke isn't able to teach people about the need to increase awareness that we can't control our pointing unless you press our hand strongly enough.

Hilke: That's probably the hardest thing for facilitators in FC writing! It is important after every letter you write to raise your hand high enough in the air (20–30 cm) to orient your hand movement in a straight line towards the letter you next intend to write. Then we, as facilitators, can sense where your index finger is heading. This requires a good deal of sensitivity on our part, especially to begin with. With every letter we have to observe ourselves to ensure we are not making any movement of our own, but are really following your movement impulse.

And in sensitively following your hand in this way, we unconsciously open our supporting hand and then you no longer feel the pressure—and therefore no longer your own hand either. Then you are unable to guide your index finger to the letter you're thinking of—and a jumble of letters results. And then both you and the facilitator give up. It really is enormously difficult for the facilitator both to follow your movement impulse sensitively and at the same time to keep remembering to press properly on your hand!

Erik: I understand the problem. But you have to teach it better.

Hilke: Is there anything else I should teach people?

Erik: That we want to have FC conversations every day.

Hilke: We others talk to each other every day after all, so this is obviously justified! But we speak with different people about all sorts of different things.

Erik: It's the same for us. We talk about mundane things with the co-workers, and about deeper things with C and you.

Hilke: Would you like to talk about deeper things with others as well? Maybe with C or me as facilitator?

Erik: We'd like to talk to everyone we meet. It is good that you invite us to do so every time.

Hilke: When we meet someone I talk to, I hold the alphabet board in front of you so that you can join in the discussion. You always have something important and interesting to say. I really try not to forget to include you. If you'd like to have conversations every day, will it be OK with mundane conversations?

Erik: It's fine, but we are more interested in deep conversations.

Hilke: Why don't you have deep conversations with the co-workers?

Erik: You can't write deeper conversations with them. They haven't meditated so they aren't very interested in what we want to talk about.

Hilke: Is there a co-worker in your residential community with whom you might have deeper conversations but who hasn't yet learned FC, and who could learn it?

Erik: No.

Hilke: So everyone should learn to meditate and then they could hold conversations with you on an equal level. Recently you wrote such good instructions for meditation.

It might be possible to give your co-workers a copy of this conversation. Perhaps one or other of them would take it further?

Erik: That's a good idea.

Hilke: Should we give it to everyone?

Erik: Many people would be able to meditate but they don't take the time they need for it. That's a shame. Their life would improve if they did. That could really do them good.

Hilke: In what way and how can meditation have this effect?

Erik: It makes us better and truer. It drives away sorrow and other difficult feelings that make life difficult.

Hilke: I'm sure it can.

Erik: It does, you know that yourself, although you don't know what your life would be like without meditation.

Hilke: I'm sure someone else, like you for instance, would be able to see and judge this better than I can.

Erik: You were never sad about having three disabled children! There are mothers who are unhappy if they just have one such child.

Hilke: You are absolutely right. One overlooks these things oneself. And because I wasn't sad about it, I have had so much pleasure with you! And it is a great joy to me now to be able to communicate with all three of you. There are indeed mothers who cannot communicate with their autistic, non-speaking child because their deep sorrow about this means they are fully convinced that their child lacks all means of advanced communication. And then they're very unlikely to be able to learn to support their children with FC. Mutual trust is essential for every real conversation.

Erik: That's true. You always believed that basically we are proper human beings! That's why it was so easy for you to learn FC.

Hilke: What does it really mean for you [plural] that you started to communicate with us about four and a half years ago?

Erik: It means we can express our wishes, and likewise our fiercely intelligent, properly intelligent views about life.

Hilke: This has really taught me a great deal! I don't succeed in fulfilling all your wishes but you have taken me with you on wonderful, indescribably enriching journeys, telling me things that no one else could have done.

Erik: You weren't Hilke in all your lives, and it wasn't good for you to be 'tubiminig' in your last life.

Hilke: What does 'tubiminig' mean?

Erik: It means 'wonderful'.

Hilke: In what language does 'tubiminig' mean wonderful?

Erik: In a language which we autistic people speak to each other in. It's a secret thing we invented. We have used it all our life, and all people with autism understand it. You yourself have seen such words many times when we've written with you.

Hilke: Yes, and then I often had to ask you the meaning of these words and you explained them. But to begin with there were so many words I didn't know that I didn't always want to ask their meaning when I understood the general content of what you had written.

Erik: You are the only one who has read such words.

Hilke: It could be hard for you to know whether the words you use yourself are ordinary Swedish words or your own ones. Tell me, do you think that autistic people in other countries, where other languages are spoken, also use your words?

Erik: I don't know.

Hilke: Can all those who can't speak as we can, hear and speak with each other?

Erik: We can.

Hilke: How good! Can you talk about everything?

Erik: We can discuss everything with each other, but we like talking about previous lives best.

Hilke: Do you all remember past lives, or do you fantasize about them?

Erik: We all remember several past lives and have no need to fantasize. This is the thing we like talking about most of all.

Sixth conversation

Hilke: Dear Erik, what do you want to pick up on in our discussion?
Erik: I want to say that we haven't been lazy while not doing anything sensible with our hands.
Hilke: Have you been able to do something else instead?
Erik: We have been able to speak about our spiritual development. You can't imagine how far one can develop if one makes an effort.
Hilke: Recently when we visited J. and his wife, you said something so beautiful. I was speaking about FC and about how far ahead of us you are in spiritual development and how much we can learn from you. Then you wrote that you are not more spiritually advanced than us but that you are becoming more spiritual because you can't speak.
Erik: That's true. We can't say a single word but we can perhaps contribute with something else that we can develop meanwhile.
Hilke: I never had any inkling of this before we were able to write with FC, but now it is quite clear to me that you can! Would you like to tell me more about this?
Erik: We can contribute with good thoughts and good advice, for instance with suggestions about how to help autistic children. We wouldn't be able to do this if we hadn't learned to use new knowledge about the extraordinarily interesting evolution of the human being.
Hilke: Can you say more about this?
Erik: I don't want to say any more about this but instead about something else. You have no idea what a good thing it is for you that you can ask us everything you wish. We can ask our spiritual advisors and they know the right answers.

Hilke: I have experienced this myself and I am grateful for it. In general we ask specialists if we need advice about all kinds of things. But your spiritual advisers can help with things that none of our specialists can answer.

Erik: You can ask any time. They really want to help with your development. Would you like to ask them anything?

Hilke: I myself used to receive personal instruction in meditation. This was really good and helped guide me in the right direction — and you sometimes remind me when I neglect it. That alone is a great help; as it is when you point me towards suitable mantras for specific situations. What should I, or we, do as a next step?

Erik: It varies, depending on the person. You could ponder on why you don't tidy your room.

Hilke: You've pointed out before how important it would be for me to tidy my desk and my room. There are piles of unsorted papers here, which need filing away under all sorts of headings. I have too little space and time, and don't keep up with things that I consider even more important. That's what I attribute this too — but maybe there's a deeper, underlying cause?

Erik: There is.

Hilke: My own inability to order things properly troubles me. What do you suggest?

Erik: You should tidy one small thing every day. Gradually you will make order. You yourself already thought of this.

Hilke: That may be the only way, for otherwise I face several days' work, and I don't have time for it.

Is there anything I can do to help you? The whole time you are trying to press all the computer keys at once with your other hand, so that it's very difficult for us to write.

Erik: You should give me more things to fiddle with.

Hilke: Is it better like this?

Erik: Yes.

Hilke: Dear Erik, why are you so restless. Is it too tiring to write so much? Or did I interfere too much and stop your hands trying to twiddle and pull and break things?

Erik: You stopped me too abruptly.

Hilke: Forgive me!

Seventh conversation

Hilke: You have just written on the alphabet board that you have a lot to write about today. I'm glad!

Erik: I would like to say that I have spoken with my spiritual advisor, and he suggested we should speak about the future of FC.

Hilke: What are his views?

Erik: He thinks that we shouldn't believe we will make headway with FC unless we have quite a number of parents on board.

Hilke: That sounds likely. So far we haven't tried to do this. I am grateful for this idea. How should we approach it?

Erik: You shouldn't approach it, but let the parents themselves take the initiative.

Hilke: What would you like to write about now?

Erik: You need to ask me.

Hilke: You mentioned that people with autism should learn to play a musical instrument. This naturally makes me think that you have been playing the marimba for many years, with very little help — well over 300 different melodies and pieces.

Erik: It's incredibly beautiful.

Hilke: For me too. Your brother Markus prefers playing the cello. I finger the notes on the fretboard and he sits to my right and plays the bow strokes by himself, the rhythms of the melodies. And I turn the cello so that his bow lands on the right string. In this way he too can play many melodies.

Erik: That's good to hear.

Hilke: Didn't you play the bowed bass* when you were a teenager?

Erik: Yes, on Saltá.

Hilke: The bowed bass is great because it is designed to be played by two people who sit opposite each other and have this large instrument lying on their knees. One person fingers the tones on a single string while the other strokes with the bow. How did you like playing this?

Erik: I didn't like it.

Hilke: Why not?

Erik: The tones were too low.

Hilke: It's true, only Markus and Andreas like these deep cello tones. You always preferred the violin, and also the recorder. Now there is a similar, smaller instrument tuned like a violin, and a still smaller one, the duoviola, with just one string. There are lines on the fretboard on which one can finger the tones, alternately with both index fingers. You can change the fretboard from diatonic to pentatonic. On the diatonic fretboard you can play ordinary melodies and songs while on the pentatonic one you can only improvise—but whatever you play always sounds beautiful.

Erik: I would have liked to play that too.

Hilke: Do you remember that there were performances on Saltá of large parts of *The Magic Flute* played on such collaborative instruments?

Erik: No, that must have been after my time.

Hilke: Yes, it must have been. But since children with autism often have an excellent feeling for rhythm, they could play on percussion instruments such as drums. What do you think of this?

Erik: It would be OK. But it's not so wonderful since they can't produce beautiful tones that way.

Hilke: And triangles?

---

* An instrument designed by Manfred Bleffert.

Erik: That's better, but still not as lovely as playing melodies.

Hilke: Do you have any further suggestions about music-making?

Erik: Getting a large orchestra together.

Hilke: What would you like to play?

Erik: Marimba.

Hilke: In the same way you play marimba you could also play xylophone, vibrophone or metallophone, or smaller chime bars.

Erik: But the marimba sounds most beautiful.

Hilke: What kind of music do you most like to hear? A large orchestra? A violin concerto? A string quartet, trio or quintet? Organ music?

Erik: I like hearing a large orchestra best.

Hilke: And what do you think autistic children like best, or what is best for them?

Erik: The same thing.

Hilke: They have a good memory. Is this also true of pieces of music they have heard? Can they hear them later on, in their memory?

Erik: Most of the children can.

Hilke: Do they also like listening to poems read aloud?

Erik: Some of them do.

Hilke: Forgive this question, but can you hear music within you once you have heard it played—for instance if you're feeling bored?

Erik: No I can't.

Hilke: When does the memory of a piece of music rise up in you?

Erik: It comes by itself, and then I feel pleased.

Hilke: It's the same for us. And then a piece of music can stay with you and keep coming back.

Erik: It's the same for us.

Hilke: You are especially musical, and sometimes I've wondered whether you compose music inside you.

Erik: I do. And my autistic friends can hear it.

Hilke: Do they like your compositions?

Erik: Yes, they value them.

Hilke: I am so pleased to hear this! Can you describe the style of your own music? Is it like that of any famous musician?

Erik: It's like Mozart and Bach.

Hilke: I feel almost envious that I can't hear your lovely music!

Erik: It's a shame since you would probably like it.

Hilke: Do you compose for a large orchestra?

Erik: Preferably for violin and orchestra.

Hilke: Did you know that only very few of us can do such a thing?

Erik: No, I didn't.

Eighth conversation

Hilke: Erik, this morning you didn't want to write but instead wished to help me tidy my room. I am very grateful to you, and I really got somewhere with it.

Now you have written that you'd like to write more about how one can help people with autism. What would you like to tell us?

Erik: One can let them do what they like without getting annoyed with them. That helps them to do it better in future.

Hilke: You have solved a riddle for me there. Recently when you pressed and hammered like mad on the keyboard with the hand we don't use for writing I was in despair and had to keep restarting the computer; and other things were happening too that I couldn't understand — and finally it stopped working altogether.

But by getting in a state and angry, I myself made the whole situation impossible, as you mentioned later. 'It just gets worse if you get angry,' you wrote on the alphabet board. And it's true: if I stay calm and accepting, it goes well. The solution to the riddle is so unexpected for me: that it isn't Erik who makes the hands do what they do!

Erik: It's true. This is my kinaesthesia-protected autism.

Hilke: That sounds very interesting and at the same time hard to understand. Can you tell me what you mean by it?

Erik: This is kinaethesia that doesn't function, so that I can't control my hands and can't speak.

Hilke: I'm starting to understand. But where does the word 'protected' come into it?

Erik: This means that I couldn't have autism if kinaesthesia functioned.

Hilke: Would you want kinaesthesia to function?

Erik: Of course!

Hilke: Is there anything else that doesn't function well, apart from kinaesthesia?

Erik: My thinking faculty.

Hilke: In what way does this function differently?

Erik: We can't think the same way as you do.

Hilke: Do you know what causes this?

Erik: It's because our brain is divided into two halves that don't work together.

Hilke: Is this so in others with autism?

Erik: Yes, in many.

Hilke: How did this come about?

Erik: I don't know.

Hilke: Do you know that it is just as hard for us to control our feelings as it is for you to control your hands?

Erik: That's difficult for us too!

Hilke: But with you [plural] I have some hard lessons to learn in this department. Do you think I'm making progress in governing my feelings, so that I don't get so angry, indignant or despairing?

Erik: You are, but you still have some way to go.

Hilke: I practise and try hard to stay calm and positive. What can I do to help you to gain control over your hands?

Erik: You can be still more relaxed.

Hilke: I will succeed in this eventually. Can the people at your workshop help you in any way? It looks as though you are trying to 'tidy up' when you put everything away and put things in different places. But you have written that this isn't so, but that you need more things to occupy you, so that you can 'arrange' them.

Erik: That's true. They should leave more things lying about everywhere.

Hilke: I will tell them. Then you wouldn't need to move all their important papers and things around everywhere, but could occupy yourself with other things. Is that what you mean?

Erik: Yes.

Hilke: At mealtimes you often don't start eating until the others have already, or almost, finished. Why is that?

Erik: It is because I first have to calm myself.

Hilke: I see. Now something quite different: How is it for autistic people to watch TV?

Erik: It's entertaining for you but not for us.

Hilke: Is there any programme that might be interesting for you?

Erik: No, we prefer looking at art books or talking to the co-workers. (The TV is often on in Erik's residential community. Some co-workers can communicate with FC.)

Hilke: Today we practised looking at some art cards with the glasses. How did you find that?

Erik: It wasn't easy, we'll have to practise.

Hilke: But your hands were still for several seconds. Then I was able to hold them for a moment, until they started trying to pull off the glasses again; and you wrote that we should take a longer break. Congratulations!

Erik: That's enough for today.

Hilke: Many thanks for today Erik!

(Immediately after this he wrote: 'I am frustrated at your stupid questions.')

Later:

Hilke: Erik, were the questions stupid because they just referred to you?

Erik: Yes, we should speak more generally.

Hilke: That's true. But that's where the conversation went, and I could imagine that such things could also be important and interesting for others.

Erik: That might be so.

Hilke: As far as children are concerned, I'd like to ask you about suitable toys. Or would it be better to speak about adults with autism?

Erik: It doesn't matter. It is impossible to talk about suitable toys.

Hilke: I was thinking of soft toys or dolls, or building blocks. I can't remember you [plural] showing any particular interest in anything like that.

Erik: This varies between different children.

Hilke: What about pictures on the walls?

Erik: That also varies. But we had a picture we liked — Madonna and Child.

Hilke: Yes, we had a large copy of Raphael's *Sistine Madonna*. You liked looking at that, even when you were still breastfeeding. Do you have any other suggestions that could be helpful for autistic children?

Erik: Long walks are good.

Hilke: Do you mean going for walks in nature?

Erik: That's best.

Hilke: Should one show them trees, flowers and animals, or do they see these anyway?

Erik: They don't see them by themselves, one has to show them.

Hilke: What do they see themselves on a walk like this?

Erik: Many things, for instance nature beings that you don't see. They speak to them in the same way you speak to each other.

Hilke: But these children cannot show us such beings because they can't speak, and we normally don't believe these beings exist.

Erik: That's true.

Hilke: But some normal children also seem to be able to see such beings, yet when they speak of them they are ridiculed and they themselves come to believe that it was just nonsense.

Erik: But we can see them all our lives.

Hilke: I didn't know that! Then you can talk about this to people who won't ridicule it.

Erik: Yes, but no one asks us.

Hilke: But now you've told me it's possible. This could turn into a long discussion.

Erik: It could if you take the time.

Hilke: I look forward to this! Perhaps during another long weekend. But now is there anything else in particular you'd like to say about children with autism and nature beings?

Erik: The nature beings would like to be in contact with you people who try to help autistic children.

Hilke: Why?

Erik: They could give you good advice.

Hilke: If the nature beings can talk to our autistic children, then they know our children better than we do!

Erik: It's true. They know how you could help each and every child.

Hilke: What can we do to stay in contact with them?

Erik: You have to take your child out into nature and sense inwardly what you feel; and you must look around very carefully to see if you feel one of these beings.

Hilke: And if we really sense the presence of one of them?

Erik: Then you can ask whether it wishes to say something about your child.

Hilke: Would it be possible to ask you or someone else who writes with FC whether you would translate such a consultation if we ourselves are too dull for such conscious contact?

Erik: This would be possible. But it would require great clairaudience on your part.

Hilke: Would we have to go out into nature together?

Erik: That wouldn't be necessary. One can invite nature beings in if one can believe in them.

Hilke: Would it be necessary for both the facilitator and parents to believe in nature beings?

Erik: Yes.

Hilke: What kind of advice can they give?

Erik: All kinds of advice. One important question for them is whether people can develop a loving relationship with each other.

Hilke: Do you mean in conversation with them?

Erik: Yes, and in general; and especially with the child. That is the most important thing.

Hilke: Are these a particular type of nature being?

Erik: They are air beings.

Hilke: Are they so loving that they concern themselves with autistic children?

Erik: They are interested in people who want to work with them.

Hilke: And are those with autism who can't speak the ones they particularly want to work with?

Erik: Yes, we work with them, but we also want to work with you [plural].

Hilke: What could this collaboration involve, apart from a concern with autistic children?

Erik: A great deal, e.g. air pollution.

Hilke: There are people who concern themselves with such things. Could they engage in unconscious collaboration with these beings?

Erik: No, they have to collaborate consciously.

Hilke: Could you also act as a translator if we could find people who were interested in this?

Erik: I could.

Hilke: Do you know anyone who would be interested?

Erik: No.

Hilke: Dear Erik, aren't you getting tired of writing so much on the computer?

Erik: I am not. It is wonderful to be able to do this.

Hilke: Then let us continue. Now, you spoke of air spirits, but there are also water spirits aren't there?

Erik: They don't concern themselves with children but with 'gimy' people.

Hilke: What are 'gimy' people?

Erik: They are people who can't behave properly because they are mentally ill.

Hilke: How do the water spirits concern themselves with these mentally ill people?

Erik: They try to use them for their own ends.

Hilke: That doesn't sound very loving.

Erik: They aren't.

Hilke: Then we ought to protect such people from them.

Erik: Yes, we can do this by making sure they don't stop long near water.

Hilke: Can you tell me why the water spirits want to exploit mentally ill people?

Erik: I don't want to tell you. You can ask me about earth beings.

Hilke: Tell me about earth beings!

Erik: They can't engage in contact with human beings but would like to know more about them.

Hilke: How can they learn more about us? In what way?

Erik: You can tell them about your childhood.

Hilke: How can I do this? I can't even see them.

Erik: You can picture them sitting in front of you and listening.

Hilke: How should I picture them—what do they look like?

Erik: They look like dwarves with pointed hats.

Hilke: Do you know how big they are?

Erik: They are no bigger than roughly the size of a hand.

Hilke: I could try to do this. How shall I know that they are listening and glad to listen?

Erik: They can give you a good feeling of wondrous joy.

Hilke: Have you tried this?

Erik: Many times.

Hilke: That is very fortunate for these beings that you have so much time and such insights.

Erik: It is fortunate that I have so much time. This is good not only for these beings but also for you [plural] for I can pray for you.

Addendum

Hilke: By the way, it is a fairly common view amongst anthroposophical curative educators that children with autism have, as it were, remained behind in the world of spirit. But several FC users have said that this isn't true of them.

One: It's exactly as you say: people think that we, who are unable to show our intelligence, have none because you [plural] can't cope with the idea that we do possess intelligence but cannot use our bodies to show these intelligent thoughts that we have all the time. But now we can write with FC and so we can show our intelligence, and contribute our capacities to culture.

Another: One has to learn a great deal of patience to endure whatever needs to be endured. We who have autism have already learned much. We can never object if what we get is not as we would wish. But now it's possible with FC. This is the best thing that has happened in our lives. What I am now able to write I used only to be able to think. Now I can communicate it to all of you. That is really wonderful. It gives meaning to my life. But I do still need patience.

3 An Autistic Person's Thoughts about Christ

Christ can come to our aid

by Hilke and Erik Osaka

Erik said this should be the title of our conversations about Christ.

During the Christmas period, Erik wanted to write about 'helping children with autism' — and this produced some astonishing conversations which can enrich the ways in which we might better understand and approach these children.

Then, one day, Erik wanted to write about Christ. What can such a disabled person know about this? It soon turned out, however, that he certainly knew and understood more than I did. We wrote about this theme from February to October 2010, interspersed with many other, private conversations.

Notes on the content of these conversations

So that the reader can better understand what Erik writes, I'll give a bit more context. A few years ago, at his own request, Erik's brother Markus attended a workshop given by Sergei Prokofieff, and afterwards wrote that he would like to attend more such events. Prompted by this, courses were arranged for adults who cannot speak at all or only very poorly. They themselves choose the lecture themes and can 'discuss' this with each other (with the aid of alphabet boards and facilitators).

After a few months they wanted to learn more about history, in particular the Nazi period, and chose the question 'How could this happen and how can we avoid it happening again in future?'

All of us were amazed that so many of them were interested in the Hitler period. They had never attended a normal school, did not like watching TV or had no access to one, and were unable to read—because they did not see well enough or were unable to turn the pages.

None of us 'normal' people wanted to engage with this terrible period, despite the increasingly insistent wish of the autistic adults. I myself still recall something from those days: the bombings, eating anything that grew in the meadows, the cold (my feet were often frozen) and the fear of the adults around me. No, I myself had absolutely no desire to know more about it.

But when we embarked on the discussions about Christ, my sons 'compelled' me to read about these events. They really wanted to know more about them and find explanations. Why? This comes out in the conversations recorded below.

Erik uses expressions that I probably need to explain. Apart from 'Christ' he mentions 'Ahriman', the adversary of the ancient Persian sun god. We might call this power 'Satan'. He seeks to draw us away from the spirit and confine us in materialism. Erik also speaks of 'Lucifer' (Latin for 'light-bringer'). This other diabolical entity tempts us towards egotism and wishes us to flee earthly hindrances. Anthroposophy teaches that we can use the influence of these two powers as the foundation for gaining freedom. We can succumb to their temptation but also fight against them, working our way towards a better and more loving future.

Erik also mentions the Lord's Prayer 'as Rudolf Steiner prayed it'. Towards the end of his life, Rudolf Steiner, the founder of anthroposophy (Greek, 'wisdom about the human being') was heard praying this loudly in his sick-room, and the version he used was written down. The 'Foundation Stone' is a longer meditative text.

I simply couldn't grasp the fact that Erik seemed to know

all this. I don't think he can have heard it from anyone. My basic stance, though, towards everything these non-speaking people write, is that I neither believe it immediately nor do I dismiss it. Maybe time will show how things really stand. For now we can regard them as interesting ideas and 'working hypotheses'. Each of us is free to form our own opinion. Meanwhile these discussions may offer new stimulus and perspectives.

I have tried the whole time not to question what Erik wrote, but just to follow it up with further questions and comments. I should probably say, also, that many of these people with autism use their own words, and I then have to ask what these words mean.

First conversation

Hilke: Erik, what would you like to tell me?
Erik: No one knows that I was born to bear witness to Christ.
Hilke: You do that with your forgiving, understanding and peaceful way of being, and with the love one can feel coming from you.
Erik: That isn't enough. I would like to write about Christ.
Hilke: Yes, please do so Erik!
Erik: I don't want to go to heaven without you. So I'd like to help you enter heaven too. For this you will need to understand Christ better.

Christ is with us always

Hilke: Erik, please say what we should better understand about Christ.
Erik: Christ is with us all the time. He doesn't impose himself. You know that he never pins you down but just waits until you ask him. Then he can help us by inspiring us with words and a little enlightenment.

Hilke: We are probably not usually attentive enough.

Erik: No, we should listen more to our intuition, as described in [Rudolf Steiner's] *The Philosophy of Freedom.* Once again, a long process of study we ought to progress more quickly with. This is taking too long — over a year and we still haven't got further than chapter three. You should tell Hans that we want to get to the chapter about moral intuition.

Hilke: It's true we haven't got very far with these studies yet; and now I wonder how you already know about this later chapter and its content.

Erik: [X] told me.

Hilke: Wonderful that you have such a far-sighted and reliable spiritual advisor! So each time that we wish to do or say something, we should check whether we might receive a Christian intuition? Is that right?

Erik: It's not necessary every time, but whenever something important is involved.

Hilke: How does one do this?

Erik: One opens oneself to Christ and comes into contact with him. Then he can show you what he himself would do in this situation. That's enough, for then we are free to act as we ourselves wish.

Hilke: Erik, that sounds very beautiful, and I wouldn't have thought of it myself. Is there anything else you'd like to say, or would you like to continue another time?

Erik: I'd like to continue another time.

Hilke: May I send this to H. and perhaps to W.?

Erik: Yes, if you remove [X]'s name and write [Y] instead.

Second conversation

Hilke: Erik, what do you want to talk about today?

Erik: I would like to write more about Christ. Especially about my best experience. The good news is that we can now be innovative in helping people with autism.

Hilke: Yes, and you yourself have made the most important contribution of all with our previous discussions.

Erik: That wasn't me but Christ.

Hilke: Then you must have worked together!

Erik: Yes, for we want to help children with autism tell their parents how much they love them.

Hilke: Was that why you wrote how important FC is for children?

Erik: It is because then they can write important things, such as when they are in pain, or when they want to see a friend or meet a good teacher.

Hilke: Yes, one can best build up good contacts when one can 'speak' together, can write with FC, if one is unable to use one's mouth to speak. I can understand this. Otherwise things stay at the level one has with a baby, or am I mistaken?

Erik: I want to speak with the people I meet, and I can do this with FC if you are there, for you always offer me the alphabet board so that I can communicate with them.

Hilke: I always used to speak aloud what you, and the others who can't speak, wrote. But you tell 'truths' that can be hard to accept for some, you say them straight out. And to be tactful I have tried to put things a little less directly. But often it has turned out that what you wanted to say can really be helpful to those you address.

Erik: You should say exactly what I write.

Hilke: Do you remember sitting next to a lady and writing that you don't want to sit next to her 'because she doesn't meditate'? I knew that she belongs to a meditation group, and so I just said: 'We should all meditate more.' She wanted to know what you had 'said', and even this was almost too much for her. She almost cringed, as though with a bad conscience. Do you understand what I mean?

Erik: I only understand it now.

Hilke: It's hardly surprising since we others have practised appropriate communication for decades, after all, and unfortunately those of you with autism have not had these years of experience. But the next time we met her you gave her such good, personal advice for her meditation practice, and she received it so gratefully!

Erik: It was nice for me to meet her again.

Hilke: Oh, she asked me to send her greetings. I'd completely forgotten.

Fighting for FC with our hearts

Erik: Can we fight for FC with our hearts? One does this by thinking positively of those who should learn to support us.

Hilke: That sounds like good advice.

You wrote on the alphabet board that your brother Andreas has a hard time. Why? Because no one in his residential community wants to write with him, and he will go under if this continues. None of us normal people could imagine what it would be like to speak with just one other person, and only for half an hour a week. His co-workers don't want to learn FC, they say they're not interested in what he might tell them! I can't insist any more than I have done. He is desperate and writes that he can't cope with it any more. What should we do?

Erik: You can think of his co-workers in a friendly way. That will help eventually.

Hilke: Thank you Erik, I'll do that.

Erik: Good people have been trying to find 'kin-questions'.

Hilke: What does 'kin-questions' mean?

Erik: Kin-questions means further means of communicating with us.

Hilke: It certainly is true that many people have tried and still try to communicate with their children, pupils or patients.

Erik: Few of them know that FC works so well.

Third conversation

Hilke: Erik, what would you like to talk about?
Erik: I want to say that I don't want to go to F (his residential community).
Hilke: I can understand this really well, but tomorrow daddy and I are going away and won't be back until Monday. You wouldn't like staying alone here.
Erik: That's true. Perhaps I could come here a bit more often.
Hilke: Let's see. At least I know now that you'd like to, and this time you have been so calm and sweet-natured!
Erik: That would be wonderful.

I didn't want to come back to earth

Hilke: Now Markus has been telling me about his experiences during the Hitler period, some of which were unimaginably awful. Is there anything you would like to tell me?
Erik: That I didn't want to come back to earth when I saw all the terrible things that happened then.
Hilke: Did you see them from heaven, or were you alive on earth at the time?
Erik: I died in a concentration camp.
Hilke: But dear Erik, that's terrible!
Erik: It was in Bergen-Belsen.
Hilke: Why were you taken there?
Erik: Because I had helped Jews to escape from a large Jewish ghetto.
Hilke: Then you yourself were not Jewish?
Erik: No, but I had many Jewish friends.
Hilke: Would you like to tell me more?
Erik: During the war I was a hero for refusing to tell the Gestapo the names of Jews I had hidden. They took me and interrogated me; and when I refused to answer they took

me and rammed several layers of gredig orcas on me until I suffocated.

Hilke: That sounds diabolical! Can you tell me what 'gredig orcas' are?

Erik: They are gredig orcas.

Hilke: Are they made of wood, or material or stone?

Erik: They are sandbags.

Hilke: May I ask whether they continued to interrogate you while they were suffocating you in such an inhumane way?

Erik: They went on doing it for ages.

Hilke: And you still managed not to tell their names?

Erik: I tried to outsmart them but it didn't work.

Hilke: Did they promise you anything if you 'collaborated' with them?

Erik: Yes, they said they'd release me. But they didn't mean it.

Hilke: Is it possible to avoid telling them what they want to hear under such inhumane treatment?

Erik: It isn't. You tell them what they want to hear, but they still kill you. But I didn't tell them all the names.

Hilke: We can't imagine not giving in under these circumstances! Then you really were a hero, and had to pay for it with your life in such a terrible way.

Erik: This was why I didn't want to come back to earth.

Hilke: How can there be people who do such inhumane things to others! I can see that this would completely deprive one of any hope of a human future! How is it that, to our great joy, you came to us despite this?

Erik: It was Christ who encouraged Markus and me.

Hilke: Did you know each other in this life during the Hitler period?

Erik: No, we knew each other from former times.

Hilke: Do you know what happened to the Jews you tried to protect?

Erik: No I don't.

Hilke: Whatever happened to them, at least they experienced someone trying to help them in a completely selfless way, in contrast to the Gestapo people. Is that right?
Erik: Yes.

Victims of the profoundest hell

Hilke: But what happened to the Gestapo people?
Erik: They can never come to knowledge of Christ. They become victims of the profoundest hell.
Hilke: Perhaps they 'deserve what they get', but is there any way of helping them? According to Christ we should turn the other cheek — do good to those who harm us and love our enemies. Is it too late for them?
Erik: You can let them be present at the Act of Consecration of Man.*
Hilke: For after all, they were human once, and then suffered brainwashing, became possessed, and were afraid that they would receive the same treatment if they didn't do what they were ordered. They caved in.
Erik: Yes, that's true.
Hilke: How do I take them with me into the Act of Consecration?
Erik: You imagine that they are standing around you.
Hilke: Does this work even if I don't know them? Or do I know any of them?
Erik: You don't know them but it doesn't matter.
Hilke: Thank you dear Erik for telling me all this! Is there anything more you would like to say?
Erik: That you believe in Christ as few others do.
Hilke: Yes, the principle of love and truth can only work on the earth through our hands or our words. Isn't that true?
Erik: It is.

---

* Part of the liturgy of the Christian Community church, founded in Switzerland in 1922.

Fourth conversation

(Before a course given by Johannes Kling on the 'threefold social organism'*)

Erik: May we have a conversation with Johannes Kling?
Hilke: He just phoned up to say that tomorrow he will first give an introductory talk lasting about half an hour, and put threefolding in a larger context. After this there will be a break for juice, and then you can put your questions and hopefully discuss them.
Erik: That sounds good. We can start with that.
Hilke: Someone ought really to write down what is said — important things might come up.
Erik: That sounds good.
Hilke: Do you already have a question you want to ask him?
Erik: Yes. Why we can't go to our insightful and productive parents and gain knowledge of threefolding from them.
Hilke: What do you think the answer would be?
Erik: They know too little about it.
Hilke: I should think that is true. And it is time that we knew more about threefolding, and its importance for the future.
Erik: That's true.

The worst period in human evolution

Hilke: You asked about the Third Reich and how the Hitler period could come about; and also how it could have been avoided. Now I have read several books about this period and about Hitler: a very disturbing read!

---

*Rudolf Steiner's ideas for a healthy society in which the three spheres of economics, justice and culture are each accorded their due domain and not subordinated to each others' laws.

Erik: This was the worst period in all human evolution.

Hilke: Yes indeed. By the way, I read that the concentration camp of Bergen-Belsen, which you referred to, lay south of Hamburg. I thought it was in Poland.

Erik: Few people know what we had to endure there.

Hilke: Many Polish Jews and also Catholics were rescued at the end of the war and brought to Sweden, and were able to tell of their experiences. All this was written down and is now in an archive in Lund. Some of their stories are in a book I borrowed from the library. I can understand why no one wants to read such things today — it is too appalling!

Erik: You should know that I wasn't there very long because I was soon killed.

Hilke: The survivors I read about were subjected to such maltreatment that they almost died. When they were half dead, beaten and tortured, they were released; and then seized once more and the whole thing started again. And throughout the years they got far too little to eat, found it hard to sleep (several people in one bed and bedbugs) and had to work so hard they nearly died.

Erik: At least I was spared all that.

Hilke: There were millions and millions of people who did not survive. Many were shot immediately (chiefly those who refused the terrible orders to afflict others) while others were gassed, having to breathe in poison gas instead of air in closed death chambers.

Erik: Hilke should soothe the hellish torments of those who did such things.

Hilke: Both you and Martin wrote of the hellish torment the tormenters must now endure. How do you think I can soothe their sufferings?

Erik: You took some of them with you to the Act of Consecration. For a while, there, you soothed their hellish sufferings. Hilke has been able to help several hundred tormenters.

Hilke: During the Hitler period people were led to believe that might is right. Christianity was disparaged, for it encourages empathy, forgiveness, and aid of the weaker by the stronger. It must be hard for them to adjust to another way.

Erik: It is logically impossible, but they can learn it in the Act of Consecration.

Hilke: I can understand that. The first few times this was so devastating that I cried throughout. You told me this was because of all their sufferings. But last Sunday I hardly cried.

Erik: They were already more cheerful.

Hilke: Can I reach enough of them?

Erik: I believe so.

Hilke: Should I continue to do this, or is there something else I should do?

Erik: You can include them in your prayers. The Lord's Prayer as Rudolf Steiner prayed it.

Hilke: Thank you Erik!

Fifth conversation

Hilke: Hello Erik, what would you like to write?

Erik: I want to write about Christ.

Hilke: Yes, I was expecting us to continue with this theme.

Erik: You were able to know that I can speak of Christ. He is the best friend we have in this life.

Hilke: Is that so?

Erik: You do not know, no one does, what Christ knows about you.

Hilke: I also experience you as such a good friend. You know me so well, and you give good advice; and also make comments that can be painful at the time but helpful in the long term if I heed them. But, dear Erik, I never experience you as being judgemental. You give esteem and love. Did you learn this from Christ?

The school of Christ

Erik: You are right. I learned all this from Christ.

Hilke: May I ask when you attended this good school?

Erik: Before I was born. The Word was there, but only few who were persecuted during the Hitler period heard it. There were many who had been persecuted but not all of them could grasp the Word because they had not previously been hell's prisoners.

Hilke: So those who had been hell's prisoners could better understand what Christ means for human beings? Is that what you mean? Can you tell me any more?

Erik: You do not know that in former times we were already hell's prisoners because we were bad.

Erik: How did we get out of this prison?

Erik: We got out of it by being born again and being persecuted ourselves.

Hilke: But surely that isn't enough to make one become a Christian, as you seem to be?

Erik: No, it isn't enough, but it needs someone to have had good thoughts about you, to have prayed for you to find your way to Christ. Someone who knew you and wished you well.

Hilke: Nowadays there aren't very many who pray such prayers, are there?

Erik: Sadly that's true. This happened in former times.

Hilke: How can we help all those today whom we don't know, who either did something bad or have been persecuted?

Erik: No one reaches Christ without desiring it himself.

Hilke: Yes, that would contradict our freedom.

Praying the Lord's Prayer every day

But how can one gain knowledge of Christ in order to seek him?

Erik: We must pray for those who are evil and those who have been persecuted; for those we read about in newspapers and see on television.

Hilke: That's a big challenge! How is it best to pray?

Erik: We can pray the Lord's Prayer for them.

Hilke: For all of them at once?

Erik: Yes, but every day.

Hilke: And do you think this can help even if there aren't very many of us who know this and who take it on as a task?

Erik: Yes. This is a great help to them when they enter the world of spirit.

Hilke: Now it occurs to me that there is no actual mention of Christ in the Lord's Prayer!

Erik: It doesn't matter. It leads them to Christ when they die.

Hilke: Is that also true of Muslims and the faithful of other religions?

Erik: Yes, they also long for Christ but call him by a different name.

Hilke: That seems understandable. Would you like to say more about Christ?

Erik: You haven't asked why we, who cannot speak, know so much more about Christ than you who generally know so much more than us.

Hilke: This was going to be my next question!

How is it that you who cannot speak know so much more about Christ than we ordinary folk? I increasingly understand what unimaginable suffering it must be to be regarded as a complete idiot: never to be able to say what you think, never to be able to express your needs and wishes or correct someone else's view.

Erik: That's true; and this helps us to take refuge in the world of spirit, where Christ comforts us. You understand us better than all others. That is why others cannot pass on much of what we wish to tell you all. You can send these conversations to whomever you like.

Hilke: Now, again, you have responded to my unexpressed question. But if there are particular people you think should read this, please give me a hint.

Erik: W and daddy.

Sixth conversation

Hilke: Hello Erik. I was very pleased to read what you wrote about Christ.

Erik: In the meantime Markus has also written with you.

Hilke: Yes, while we were in Paris. He didn't write so much about Christ in general, but instead gave specific advice for certain people.

Erik: He did not write about people who [think they] do not need to know about Christ. But that's something I can, and want to do.

Hilke: Yes, people need to know what you can tell us!

Erik: More people need to pray to the Father.

Hilke: In what way Erik?

Erik: The way you pray with Markus.

Hilke: I usually pray the normal Lord's Prayer with you. Markus wanted us to pray it in the version Rudolf Steiner gave. In Paris we first prayed it in German, and then he wanted to pray it in Swedish.

Erik: The best is Rudolf Steiner's version. It's best in German, but it's also good in Swedish.

Hilke: And Martin said that one should copy it down by hand.

Erik: That's right.

Hilke: Can one give this to absolutely anyone?

Erik: Yes, it's applicable to all.

Hilke: Do you want to say more about it?

Erik: No.

Seventh conversation

Erik: I want to write about Christ again. That is the most important thing at present.

Hilke: I'd be very pleased Erik!

Erik: Christ is always with us.

Hilke: With all people or only certain ones?

Erik: With all. We are all one in Christ.

Hilke: Isn't it very painful for him to live in such close proximity to people who still live with the pre-Christian attitude of 'an eye for an eye, a tooth for a tooth'? Revenge instead of forgiveness. And all the evil that seduces us.

Erik: Christ can endure broken promises and other stupid judicial chemical atrociousness; but not the I-egotism of audacious people. This destroys our heavenly portion.

Only loving oneself

Hilke: How does the 'I-egotism' of people express itself? Can you give me any examples?

Erik: I-egotism has many faces. It is clear that one cannot come to pleasant places in heaven if one cannot love at all. But the worst thing is that one cannot be released from hell if one doesn't succeed in overcoming one's I-egotism there. Then one is lost to human evolution.

Hilke: So there seems to be a difference between ordinary egotism and I-egotism?

Erik: There's a big difference: ordinary egotism does not mean one cannot love. But I-egotism means one cannot love anything other than oneself.

Hilke: Not even such things as nature, or animals, or the truth?

Erik: No, absolutely nothing.

Hilke: Do you think there are such people today?

Erik: Yes, unfortunately.

Erik: Do we know any of them?

Erik: No, they are somewhere else. They cannot be born now, so as to learn more. They will increase in number if Christianity does not spread further. Then the earth will go under. We must learn to become loving.

Hilke: It's true, Erik, we have to learn that.

Now I have to make lunch, and I look forward to writing more afterwards, and hearing all the new things you're telling me.

Now we can carry on talking.

Erik: We can't gain understanding of heaven if we don't fathom the I and come to a view of what it really is. The I is a good, reliable heavenly help on the path towards proper evolution. The heavens know that we need the I for our evolution. But this must be transformed into selflessness, otherwise we won't get any further.

Hilke: And here the Christian message comes into its own surely?

Erik: Yes. With the help of the Christian message we can transform our egotism into selflessness.

Hilke: Now I understand Waldorf education better. The children have so many activities—academic subjects, all sorts of artistic activities, various kinds of craft and hand-work—so that all children can shine in one area at least and don't need to compete with each other; instead they can learn to help each other to improve. And there's no competition involving marks and test scores.

Erik: That's right.

Hilke: Is there anything we normal people can do to help each other towards the goal that you have described?

Erik: You know yourself that we must work together to help arrange life in accordance with the threefold idea.

Hilke: Can you say more?

Erik: Economic life should only produce what people need, and no one should become richer by driving others out of business. The best people for the job should direct companies but not own their capital. No one apart from teachers themselves should interfere in teaching and what is taught, and cultural life should be fully independent.

Hilke: And the state?

Erik: Laws should be created by the people themselves.

Hilke: At present laws are made by members of parliament, parties elected by people.

Erik: Laws must be created by referenda.

Hilke: Last week, Markus and I attended a wonderful concert in Paris, in Saint Chapelle, which is formed almost entirely of high, beautiful, medieval stained glass windows. To get there you have to pass through the court buildings, over whose entrance, in large letters, stand the words 'liberté, egalité, fraternité'. And now you are describing fraternity in economic life, equality amongst human beings in relation to laws, and independence, and freedom of cultural life!

Erik: That's how I understand the threefold social order. We need to become fraternal in relation to natural resources and their processing and distribution. We must become free and creative in relation to the life of the mind and spirit; and we must be able to feel ourselves equal in order to judge which laws we need.

Hilke: These are huge insights. How did you come to them?

Erik: Kling said some things, and Martin explained the rest.

Hilke: Then you and Martin could become our teachers!

Erik: But we can't speak.

Hilke: That's true, sadly, but you can write so well with FC, unexpectedly and incredibly. May I ask whether Martin can tell the others who were present at Johannes Kling's talk about his insights?

Erik: He has done.

Hilke: How shall we continue now? Or is there anything more you'd like to say before we drive back to F?

Erik: I don't want you to give this to [A].

Hilke: OK. May I send it to I? W? Johannes Kling? May daddy read it?

Erik: You can give it to anyone you like.

Hilke: Thank you dear Erik! And I look forward to further conversations. You have so much of great importance to teach us ordinary people, who always thought we were so much cleverer than all you who have autism. Yes, without FC we would no doubt have retained that belief.
Erik: I'll be glad to come here again and tell you more.
Hilke: Great!

Eighth conversation

Hilke: Hello Erik, what would you like to write?
Erik: I want to go on writing about Christ.
Hilke: I'm pleased!
Erik: Christ is in all of us and we are in him. Children are more open for this, but we who can't speak can also be more open for him.
Hilke: At least there's one benefit, then, in your sad destiny of being unable to speak. So children are more open to Christ.

You have crucified Christ with your egotistic thinking

Why are we ordinary adults no longer so open to him?
Erik: Because you have been able to crucify him again. You have crucified Christ with your egotistic thinking.
Hilke: At Golgotha, it is said, Christ resurrected to eternal life through his own power.
Erik: He can still do so now if we learn to pray properly for help so that Jesus can participate in our heart's thinking.
Hilke: Is there a special prayer for this, or how should we do this?
Erik: We can pray the Lord's Prayer as Rudolf Steiner prayed it.
Hilke: Yes, because this was Jesus' own prayer to his Father, we can as it were pray it with him. That is what I have thought in the past, but I'm not sure if it's right.

Erik: It is right.

Hilke: Thank you! You have written that, apart from little children you too, who can't speak, are more open to Christ. Do you know if this is also true of others who can't express themselves in speech but who don't have autism. I'm thinking of such conditions as Rett syndrome, cerebral paresis, brain damage following a traffic accident, or non-speaking Down's syndrome, etc. Are such people also closer to Christ?

Erik: It varies. Most but not all.

Ninth conversation

The reversed Lord's Prayer and the Act of Consecration

Hilke: Hello Erik. Today is Sunday and we have the whole afternoon to ourselves.

Erik: Mummy has been able to take many unfortunate people with her into the Act of Consecration.

Hilke: I tried inviting many, and it is lovely to know that you experienced some of them being present there. Did I do this right or can I do it still better?

Erik: There's room for improvement. You can pray the Prayer of Knowledge for them.

Hilke: Which prayer is that?

Erik: It is the reversed Lord's Prayer, with which Rudolf Steiner nourished the earth when the foundation stone for the first Goetheanum was laid.

Hilke: You have written that he 'nourished the earth' with this [in Swedish more literally 'fed'].

Erik: Yes, he fed the earth with it. It was the earth that needed to hear this.

Hilke: Tell me more!

Erik: This was an extraordinary new help for the earth to hear this.

Hilke: Should I pray this for the tormenters and those they tortured to death alongside the Lord's Prayer, for example before it or after it? Or should it be during the act of worship?

Erik: You can pray it each morning before the Lord's Prayer.

Hilke: I will try to do so. I'm sure I can find this 'reversed' Lord's Prayer. I'm so glad you want to help me! Can these unfortunate people absorb the message of the Act of Consecration?

Erik: Yes.

Hilke: How good! And then I want to say that you were able to be so calm and still during this service!

Erik: I was able to be calm a long time, but not the whole time.

Hilke: Is there anything I can do in future to help you to be calm and still?

Erik: No, you already help me by being calm yourself.

Hilke: Is there anything else you'd like to say?

Erik: I'd like to go every Sunday.

Hilke: We'll try to do this. What should we do about Z, who held the service today? He can't believe that you are ordinary, clever people who recall their past lives and can have deeper insights into the spiritual world than we normal ones. He believes that I myself am writing all these things in a kind of mediumistic way.

Erik: He will be better able to understand if you let him read what I have written about helping autistic children.

Hilke: The first of these conversations?

Erik: Yes, that's best.

Hilke: A really good, sensible idea!

Tenth conversation

Hilke: Hello, dear Erik, what would you like to say?

Erik: I want to say more about Christ. Hilke wasn't able to practise taking communion with me.

Hilke: In Paris, at his 'little church', Markus wanted to be present and take part in communion. But then he regretted it, and wrote that this was no longer appropriate for him, and that instead he wanted to take communion in the Christian Community. He suggested that we should ask a priest to hold the Act of Consecration for you, who are not usually allowed to be present because you 'disturb' the service. And then it occurred to me that you should receive some kind of confirmation classes as children otherwise do before their first communion.

Erik: That is a good idea, but first we must practise taking the bread and wine, so that we don't drop it.

Hilke: That is what happened a few years ago when we tried to come forward to receive communion. After the service the priest found a small piece of bread on the ground, and after that no longer wanted any of you to receive communion. At the time I understood that no one had explained to you what happens; and now I see that we should first practise with ordinary bread and juice.

Erik: You're right, we need more preparation.

Hilke: Is anything else needed?

Erik: We should hear something about the structure of the Act of Consecration, and how Christ can come to us through communion.

Hilke: You have been present at the Act of Consecration on several occasions, and have watched people receiving communion. Have you experienced the transformation of the bread and wine into 'Christ's body' and 'Christ's blood', or what happens during communion?

Erik: No, I was unable to experience anything in particular except that Christ was present.

Hilke: If we can get a priest to hold a preparatory meeting with you, and agree to hold a service for you, who would be interested in taking part?

Erik: I, Markus and Andreas and Martin and at least seven others, and also the F. co-workers.

Eleventh conversation

Hilke: Hello Erik, what would you like to say today?

Erik: I'd like to say that you meditated well. You also meditated on the Prayer of Knowledge. That was a good deed.

Hilke: Yes, I was able to find it, and in this context it felt really intense. Now I remember that Rudolf Grosse once said in a lecture that this prayer takes us down to the deepest abyss, beyond which one cannot fall any further. At the same time, by recognizing and experiencing the 'very bottom', this means one can only rise upwards once more, as I now understand.

Erik: That may be so, as long as one does not stay there.

Hilke: Let us hope that as many as possible turn their path back in an upward direction!

Erik: Yes, let us hope this.

Hilke: But you probably realize how astonished I still am when you know so precisely what I have meditated on, and how successful or not I have been. You were sleeping in the adjacent room—I heard you snoring—and I said nothing out loud. But I do not feel you were 'eavesdropping'. I experience, rather, your warm desire to help.

Erik: I know what you are thinking.

Hilke: But I myself do not know something like this—whether I managed it well and what it means for others.

Erik: Christ tells me it, at least when it will help someone else.

Former Nazis present at the service

Hilke: Martin wrote that, after death, when we experience how we have made others suffer, the Nazi oppressors undergo indescribably terrible torments; that they have landed in hell and remain imprisoned there. It was you, Erik, who suggested I take them with me into the Act of

Consecration, and then you explained to me why I was crying there the whole time, experiencing their awful suffering.

Erik: That's so.

Hilke: And Martin wrote that I must now carry on with this, for otherwise they will sink downwards again, and that would be worse than if I had never started. He said they could drag me down with them, and only Christ could save me again at Easter. Do you think I understood this aright?

Erik: You did.

Hilke: Then I also invite them to the Lord's Prayer, and this feels very right with the 'reversed' Lord's Prayer, to which you drew my attention.

Erik: You're right, you should continue with it.

Hilke: Yesterday after the service you wrote that many of them were present.

Erik: That's right. There were thousands.

Hilke: You also suggested that I could take with me those who have been tormentors since then, and right up to now. And of course I also invite the victims. I simply do this as well as I can, by picturing a few whose suffering I have heard or read about; and by feeling open to them. Is that good?

Knocking at the gates of hell

Erik: You can do still more by going to hell and asking for permission to take them with you.

Hilke: How does one do this?

Erik: One goes to the gates and knocks.

Hilke: How does one get to these gates — I can't see them. Should I first think of the Prayer of Knowledge?

Erik: No, you shouldn't go to the gates of hell. You aren't able to do this yet.

Hilke: Thomas [another autistic adult] wrote that I should also invite the souls who have got even more stuck and now work against humanity in Ahriman's service, negatively influencing us all the time. They are souls who expunged the Knights Templar for their own advantage, and also some from the Hitler period. But Martin wrote that this is too dangerous for me, that I can't manage this. So I have left it.

Erik: You must leave that to Martin.

Hilke: Martin also explained my own karmic background, which now leads me to help. Not a pretty story!

Erik: And you shouldn't tell anyone else about it.

Hilke: No, it is easy to leave it: to let it be!

Twelfth conversation

Contacting one's own angel

Hilke: Hello Erik, what would you like to speak about today?

Erik: I'd like to speak more about Christ.

Hilke: Gladly!

Erik: We have to know that there is a way for us to achieve understanding with the aid of our good friend, our angel.

Hilke: The question is how we manage to do this.

Erik: If one desires the help of one's angel, then one can come into contact with him. And then he can explain the workings of Christ in one's own life.

Hilke: I didn't know this, and therefore never tried it. Most people find it difficult to conceive that we each have our own angel.

Erik: We do, but he holds back in order to leave us free.

Hilke: How can we sense him or know about him?

Erik: We can do this by looking at our own lives and reflecting on the different people who have meant something to us; and by seeing how such meetings came about. Here we can see the help of our angel.

Hilke: Then he is the one who knows what will be important for our development as a human being?

Erik: Yes, he is the one who leads me to whoever is significant for me.

Hilke: And then it is up to me to have a sense of this person's qualities?

Erik: That's right. You don't know you need this person before you meet him.

Hilke: Is this also true of people who are unkind or unfriendly, or even harm us?

Erik: Those are often the ones who are most important for our development.

Hilke: But surely not if they destroy us?

Erik: Your angel helps you by buoying you up again.

Hilke: So if for example one 'gets a grip on oneself' instead of, say, sinking into alcoholism, this can succeed through the help of our angel even if we know nothing about this?

Erik: Yes. If we get this kind of help then it is always our angel who has helped us.

Hilke: What you write here can really help me to be aware of my angel, and thereby perhaps to make contact with him.

Erik: You have already started to make contact with him by asking him each evening to help you meditate more deeply.

Hilke: I did this on your advice, and it seems to help, but so far it is still a more unconscious contact.

Erik: It's a good beginning. Perhaps, now that you have started to meditate more deeply, you will also be able to experience your angel. You can also meditate with him.

Hilke: A long time ago someone told me that I can feel addressed by my angel as 'human soul' whenever I meditate on the Foundation Stone verses. Recently, though, it felt to me as though several spiritual beings were calling these verses out to me.

Erik: The hierarchies call them out to us.

Hilke: So we should listen more attentively.

Erik: With your attentiveness you will soon be able to hear them. You can really already hear them.

Hilke: I'm sure you still have more to write. Or should we stop now?

Erik: It is a beautiful thing to discuss such far-reaching things. You make it easy for me to express myself.

Hilke: May I ask how I make it easy for you?

Erik: By supporting my hand. And by asking sensible questions. You make it easy for me to write good things.

Hilke: I thank you for that. But in fact I only put questions that follow on from what you write. The important thing for me is that you can say what you yourself want, things you can't say by any other means. Then you always show me when it is my turn to respond.

Erik: You didn't meditate at midday today.

Hilke: It's true. Do you think it would be best if I do it now, at a quarter past eight in the evening, or before I go to sleep? Or shall I leave it now?

Erik: You can do it before you go to bed.

Hilke: Thank you for reminding me.

Thirteenth conversation

Hilke: Hello Erik, what would you like to tell me?

Erik: I want to write about Christ. He wishes to help us have confidence in each other.

Hilke: Such help is greatly needed!

(Then he wrote some very personal advice and thoughts.)

Fourteenth conversation

Hilke: Hello Erik, what would you like to say?

Erik: I want to work hard to develop real knowledge of Christ. One can do this by meditating on Christ a little each day.

Hilke: With a prayer or a mantra, or a thought or a question...?

Erik: I suggest one should learn a way in which one can continue to work each day. That is, by reading a little of the Bible every day.

Hilke: That's a very good suggestion! I assume that you mean the New Testament with the Four Gospels. Is there a particular Gospel you would recommend?

Erik: The Gospel of St John.

Hilke: Yes, that is the most spiritual Gospel, with the simplest language. It was the Gospel upon which the Cathars founded their lives.

Erik: They were good people unable to inflict any harm on another. They could teach us how we can live peacefully together.

Hilke: I admire them so much with their pure teachings, their selflessness, their humility and capacity for love. Markus has told us about how people tried to convert them to Catholicism because of fears that Islam would conquer all Europe if Christianity was not united.

Erik: That's true. But then they were burned alive, and that was a bad action.

Hilke: Was Pope Innocent III guilty of this?

Erik: No, Innocent III wanted to convert them.

Hilke: I do not know if this theme we have now broached was one you wanted to write about.

Erik: He really did wish to save Christianity.

Hilke: This is a point of view I never remember hearing or reading about when daddy and I were in the land of the Cathars, and were reading about them. But it gives a more understandable context to their whole persecution!

Fifteenth conversation

Blazing for Christ

Hilke: Hello Erik, it's late now, but you'd like to write something.

Erik: I want to say that we have to start blazing for Christ.

Hilke: How do we do this?

Erik: By praying to him to let all good people come to him.

Hilke: I'm not sure I understand this. Won't he let them come to him otherwise?

Erik: No, he waits until they themselves want this.

Hilke: Isn't that enough?

Erik: No, they can't come to him because they don't know about him.

Hilke: Do you mean he should become more active and not just wait for them?

Erik: Yes, that's what I mean.

Hilke: But what about their freedom?

Erik: There's no problem, for they can refuse to come.

Hilke: That's true. Let us hope that we can ask him intensively enough for him to respond to this. It seems necessary.

Erik: It really is necessary.

Hilke: You wrote on the alphabet board that it isn't easy to be disabled, and that it isn't Christ who wants you to be, but Ahriman. Do you want to say any more about this?

Erik: That's just how it is.

Hilke: But there's something I wonder about. If you weren't disabled but were the same as us ordinary folk, would you still have the spiritual insights which we don't have?

Erik: We could still have them and work for spiritual evolution.

Hilke: How did Ahriman gain power over you?

Erik: When Hitler had us tortured to death.

Hilke: How did Hitler gain such power?

Erik: He got it from 'minimal' people.

Hilke: What are 'minimal' people?

Erik: People who didn't know how evil he was.

Hilke: And who let him take all the power, presumably. Was he led astray and governed by evil forces?

Erik: Yes. He was inspired by evil forces, and then hell gained a purchase on us. We no longer wished to participate in human evolution; but Christ asked us to be reborn. But we were unable to develop our nervous system sufficiently.

Hilke: Why couldn't you?

Erik: Because we were unable to know enough about it.

Hilke: Is it because you were born again so soon?

Erik: No, it was because Ahriman stopped us knowing how it is done.

Hilke: Do people who are going to be born otherwise learn from Ahriman how to build up their nervous system?

Erik: No, but he hinders us from learning it.

Hilke: Were you too despairing because of the terrible way you were killed?

Erik: Yes, we were in too much despair to get past Ahriman.

Hilke: May I ask if this is true of many people with autism?

Erik: Yes, it's true of most of them.

Hilke: It sounds so shocking that Ahriman, with Hitler's help, was able in this way to obstruct a more light-filled development of civilization, by preventing spiritual people, in particular, from being heard.

Erik: That's true.

Hilke: Do you want to go to bed now, or write some more? Shall we continue tomorrow?

Erik: We can write more tomorrow.

Sixteenth conversation

Hilke: It's a new day, and you'd like to continue.

Erik: We can't reach Christ if we don't walk side by side.

Hilke: How do we walk side by side?

Erik: We have to walk together, go hand-in-hand.

Hilke: But don't we already need Christ's help to be peaceful and forgiving enough to manage to go hand-in-hand?

Erik: That is true. But in order to get further, more is needed.

Hilke: Surely there are already some of us who try to walk hand-in-hand?

Erik: It doesn't yet work with all. You can regret the fact that you haven't yet got [A] and [B] on your wavelength.

Hilke: If I must regret it then that must mean that I did it wrong or made too little effort.

Erik: You did what you could.

Hilke: Then perhaps I don't have to be regretful but sad and disappointed; but I can try in future to walk hand-in-hand with them towards the same goal, can't I?

Erik: Christ wants you to work together.

Hilke: Many thanks for letting me see that this really ought to happen.

Praying to God

Erik: You can't know that you no longer have to go to God to continue to courageously accentuate what is good.

Hilke: That sounds as though, usually, one has to go to God.

Erik: That is so.

Hilke: How does one do that?

Erik: One prays to God for illumination about how to think in this respect.

Hilke: Can I ask you what you mean when you say that I myself no longer need to do this?

Erik: It's because you pray to God every day anyway.

Hilke: Yes, I understand this better now. Why was it that I couldn't get A and B on my wavelength?

Erik: It's because they don't go to God every day.

Hilke: Is it Rudolf Steiner's Lord's Prayer, or ... meditation, or the Foundation Stone?

Erik: The Lord's Prayer.

Hilke: And I would never have taken this up if you and

Martin had not persuaded me to understand how important that is!

Erik: That's so good!

Hilke: Markus and I met a man at Chartres Cathedral whom Markus said was a modern initiate. Did Markus tell you this?

Erik: He did. We want to meet him.

Hilke: Now I have written an email to this man saying we would like to meet him in Sweden (both Markus and Andreas wrote this) and he has written back to say he would like to come here with his friend, whom we also met, and the latter's girlfriend. They're going to see when they can come.

Erik: That was the most important thing for Markus on the whole trip.

Hilke: It also was for me. I have never seen such a selflessly loving and understanding person, attentively listening and encouraging.

Seventeenth conversation

Understanding anthroposophy better

Erik: It will soon be necessary to come to a better understanding of anthroposophy.

Hilke: How can we better understand anthroposophy?

Erik: We must take its content to our hearts.

Hilke: How can we do that better?

Erik: By asking Christ to help us.

Hilke: To help with what?

Erik: To become Christians.

Hilke: We would gladly learn to become Christians, but how can we do so?

Erik: We can do this by helping future generations.

Hilke: How can we help future generations?

Erik: By praying the Lord's Prayer as Rudolf Steiner prayed it.

Hilke: Is this part of anthroposophy?

Erik: It belongs intrinsically to it!

Hilke: So you mean it is not enough to understand the deed of Christ, as anthroposophy describes it, only through our heads?

Erik: It is fine to understand it, but we must also pray to Christ.

Hilke: But the Lord's Prayer is not directed to Christ.

Erik: That doesn't matter. We pray it together with Christ, as you already saw.

Hilke: Is this enough for becoming Christian?

Erik: Yes. One should pray it every day.

Hilke: Rudolf Steiner himself apparently prayed it every day his whole life long.

Eighteenth conversation

Hilke: Hello Erik, what would you like to say?

Erik: I would like to say that you should hear what Christ has to tell you about my destiny and all that happened at the concentration camp. You can't understand how terrible this was.

Hilke: You are right. Now I have read five books about the Hitler period. It is so appalling that one just can't imagine such inhumanity.

Erik: You have no idea how terrible it was to be slowly suffocated to death.

Hilke: I imagine it must have been just as terrible, at least, to experience the inhumanity of those who did this. Without any empathy — but its absolute opposite. Were they cynical or did they actually enjoy torturing others?

Erik: They were cynical.

Hilke: It's enough to make you lose all faith in humanity!

I didn't want to be reborn

Erik: That's true. I didn't want to be reborn, but Christ persuaded me to stay part of human evolution.

Hilke: My very greatest thanks to him for that! Such people as you are ones in whom we can place our hope that evolution can progress towards greater love and human understanding.

Erik: That's true, but the memories are so awful.

Hilke: We who never experienced it ourselves can only have an inkling of this. Just reading about these atrocities leaves me haunted by them.

Erik: It is good that you try to understand. That helps us to get over these things.

We experienced hell on earth

Hilke: I didn't know that. The Third Reich was a whole, terrible system. All those who interrogated others in the most appalling way and tortured them to death—as they did to you—knew that if they didn't do this as their superiors demanded they would suffer the same fate as their victims. Even those who were in the upper echelons close to Hitler would have been executed if they hadn't joined in with the evil. It seems they felt compelled to outdo each other in evil deeds. And they knew the terrible things that would happen to them otherwise. Thus Satan and the devil were given a free hand to ensnare human beings. Is that right?

Erik: That's how it was. We experienced hell on earth. It could not have been more diabolical.

Hilke: Now we can hope that all have learned a lesson, those like you who suffered this cruelty but also the perpetrators when, after death, they had to experience what they had made you suffer. I can imagine it must be even worse for them.

Erik: That's true. It was even worse for them. And now they don't know how they can undo what happened. They wish so fervently that it had never happened.

Hilke: One can understand this so very well!

Erik: This must never happen again.

Hilke: So have all now learned their lesson?

Erik: Sadly not. The worst ones among them now serve Ahriman* and work for the extermination of the whole human race.

Hilke: This is entirely in accord with the aims of the Hitler elite. First all those who weren't German (inferior races) and then, towards the end, Hitler thought the Germans had been so ineffective in his war that they might as well be destroyed as well. But what use is it to Ahriman if the whole of humanity is eradicated?

Erik: I do not know. (*Refuses to write more.*)

Hilke: Do you think that victims during the Nazi period have the strength to forgive their tormentors?

(*He writes on the alphabet board:* I don't want to write any more, it's too frightening.)

Later he wrote: You should not think that you are better than those who killed Christ. *After I'd recovered a little from this comment, I said I was very glad I was a baby and infant during the Nazi time, because I'm sure I wouldn't have been any better than anyone else. And don't we crucify Christ every day by some of what we do or say? Erik agreed, and wrote that we would be arrogant if we didn't realize this.*

Nineteenth conversation

Death in the concentration camp

Hilke: Hello Erik, what would you like to write before the concert? (*We had arrived almost an hour too early.*)

---

*Editors' note: In fact, as we will see later, the figure referred to as 'Ahriman' is Sorath. We left the name Ahriman to preserve the actual wording of the text.

Erik: I want to write about my experiences in the concentration camp.

Hilke: Erik, I'd like to know about them.

Erik: It wasn't a laughing matter. It was really dreadful. We got nothing to eat, only water and a little bread. I did not want to say where my friends the Jews were hidden. They pressed me to the ground under sacks of sand and I couldn't get any air and suffocated.

Hilke: One can't imagine such a situation, so awful!

Erik: I remember them asking and asking me, but they were never satisfied with my answers.

Hilke: That sounds as if there were quite a few of them?

Erik: There were more than three.

Hilke: Did they all interrogate you?

Erik: No, just one of them asked the questions while the others listened and were cynical.

Hilke: Do you think they would have let you go if you had told them straight away where your friends were hidden?

Not wanting to be born again

Erik: I don't believe so, but at the time I thought they would release me if I betrayed them. They got me to betray them and then suffocated me anyway. That was the worst of all. I could not endure it, and did not wish to be born again.

Hilke: In such a situation one can't conceal anything. I can imagine that it's not because one is afraid to die but because one loses all composure when suffering such torture.

Erik: Such torture means that one no longer knows what one is doing. It's the very worst thing there is. They knew this and exploited it.

Hilke: Do you know how long this lasted?

Erik: Perhaps four hours. But it felt like an eternity. It was like a long drawn-out battle to the death. They tortured me for a very long time, especially slowly so as to enjoy my torment. It was so hugely cynical—no one can understand it.

Hilke: Under normal circumstances no ordinary person can understand this. It sounds to me as though you didn't want to be born again not so much to escape such suffering in a new life but because you couldn't endure the fact that you betrayed your friends. May I ask if that's so?

Erik: It was as you say.

Hilke: Martin told us that in his next life, that is now, he did not want to be able to speak, so that no one could ever force him again to commit misdeeds against others.

Erik: I didn't want to be able to betray my friends again.

Hilke: But it is so inconceivably atrocious that you first had to endure these experiences during the Hitler period, and now you have such a disability, one so hard to endure.

Erik: It wasn't I who did something wrong but Ahriman.

Hilke: So Ahriman has done two things 'wrong'. First he inspired people to set up an inhuman, evil system, and then he prevented you from properly developing your nervous system in this life.

Erik: Yes. You cannot believe how terrible this is. If I don't get help from you I won't be able to return.

Hilke: Why won't you be able to come back again—and how can we help you?

Erik: We have to understand Christ better, and you must learn to give us new faith in humanity.

Hilke: How can we give you faith in humanity?

Erik: You can do this by doing what you can to give us love.

Hilke: I have told you that I am glad I was a young child during the Hitler period. If I had been an adult, I do not know if I could have resisted this evil. And to betray one's friends under these circumstances is unthinkable.

Twentieth conversation

Hilke: I have pondered a long time on something in our conversation yesterday. It is the idea that one suffers so terribly at the time of Hitler and then is severely disabled with autism in one's next life. I cannot come to terms with the idea that one might not be born again as a result. Some people with autism, with whom I have written, want to learn important things in this life such as the threefold social organism, precisely so they can help improve things in their next life.

Erik: That's true, but not self-evident. You spoke with those who can come back because Christ helps them. But others cannot because they get no proper help.

Hilke: Why don't they get proper help?

Erik: It is because their 'I' did not seek Christ while they were being tortured to death.

Hilke: In what way can one seek Christ while one is being so badly tortured? And can one do this if one doesn't belong to any Christian religion?

Erik: Instead of focusing on the guilt of the torturers, one regards them as victims too. People of other religions can do this as well.

Hilke: This sounds formidable and I wonder how many people who now have autism can be so selfless.

Erik: There were many of them.

Hilke: And they can come back to a new life on earth?

Erik: Yes, if they now get help from Christ.

We can't forgive your arrogance

Hilke: What do you think this depends on if they now get this help or not?

Erik: It depends on whether they can forgive their parents for all the stupid things they do.

Hilke: And we parents do so many stupid things to you, especially before we can understand you through FC. Even if, as parents, we believe that deep within you are healthy, we often still treat you in such impossible and humiliating ways!

Erik: That's true.

Hilke: Can we do anything to enable these people with autism to forgive us? We others inflict such cruelty on you in pure desperation.

Erik: We can forgive most of what you do, but not your arrogant belief that we are worth far less than you.

Hilke: This madness was most widespread during the Hitler period. Is it still so widespread?

Erik: Not in Sweden but in other countries.

Hilke: That's true. There are countries where autistic people are hidden away all their lives. They aren't even allowed to leave their home. But their relatives, who are so ashamed, also suffer a lot from this.

Erik: That's right. And these children can try to forgive their parents.

Hilke: When are they unable to forgive them?

Erik: When the parents give them away to die.

Hilke: I didn't know that such things happen. Just think what these parents lose—and they don't even know it. There are many children with Down's syndrome and other disorders which are diagnosed while the mother is still pregnant. Often these foetuses are aborted so that their souls cannot embark on this life.

Erik: Then they are born in another body.

Hilke: I am so relieved to hear that you think this doesn't apply to all of these.

Erik: That was all for today.

Twenty-first conversation

Experiencing Christ's love

Hilke: Hello Erik, what shall we talk about?

Erik: We can speak about Christ. We have to understand that Christ is always in us. We just need to become aware of this.

Hilke: What must we become aware of here? How can we recognize him?

Erik: We do this through a feeling of calm and peace. And a feeling of love which we can experience repeatedly if we are attentive.

Hilke: I have experienced moments when I felt enormously loved, but I could not fathom by whom.

Erik: That was the love of Christ.

Hilke: But it felt very personal. Recently, whenever I felt really badly treated I have made efforts to forgive, quite simply to have some understanding, and then I experienced how love could quite unexpectedly emanate from me.

Erik: Here too you experienced Christ's love.

Hilke: I am so glad and grateful to hear you say this! So now I will risk asking you whether you know of other opportunities for me to discover Christ's working within me. The feeling I mentioned only rarely occurs.

Erik: When you meditate, for example, and notice that you can concentrate well.

Hilke: Unfortunately I don't find it so easy, but it's true that a good feeling does arise. Tell me, are there also occasions in daily life where something like this occurs?

Erik: When you find that you get a good idea about doing something for someone else.

Hilke: Great! That does happen now and then.

Erik: You can also feel you are managing to support us without knowing what exactly we are going to write about next. There too Christ can help us to write what we ourselves wish.

Hilke: That's not so easy. Our brain automatically tries to finish every word and sentence we begin, and really also the whole train of thought. I found the first supplementary exercise* was a prerequisite during our conversations for stopping my own train of thoughts while I was supporting you, and only thinking about what had been written after you'd written it, and it was my turn to respond.

Erik: You're the best at this.

Hilke: I can imagine there must be other opportunities as well in daily life.

Erik: If you can be attentive to your thoughts you'll notice that you cannot know when you will have ideas about Christ. They come when you least expect. Then they come from Christ.

Hilke: I will try to pay attention to this. I have accustomed myself in fact to attending to others' wishes and to realizing them if possible. That feels satisfying and good. But couldn't this involve a certain amount of laziness: letting others decide and not being so active oneself by initiating things?

Erik: Christ wants us to relate to each other like that.

Hilke: I find that very comforting. As far as the trips are concerned that I undertake with those of you who can't speak, it has become clear that the more thoroughly and frequently I ask you what we should do and how, and the more conscientiously I follow your wishes, the better the trip goes. But then it is you who have deeper insights than I do.

Erik: That's right. For our part we can ask our spiritual advisors for help, and we get good advice from them.

Hilke: And they seem to have a better overview than we do.

Erik: Yes, you're quite right.

Hilke: And they seem to wish to help us others if we have important questions and you act as 'translators'.

Erik: That's right. They really want to help, but they don't try to impose themselves.

---

* Concentrating on an object and developing thoughts about it in a clear sequence.

Hilke: That strikes me as a genuinely Christian stance. And it's something you already wrote about during our first conversation. By contrast, evil and disruptive beings seek to impose themselves.

Erik: That's the difference. That's how we can distinguish between Ahriman and Christ.

Hilke: But Lucifer also imposes himself, doesn't he? Or is that different?

Erik: Yes, he does not wish to be discovered and here he can work hand-in-hand with Ahriman.

Lucifer prevents people from meditating

I had a conversation with my cousin from Tasmania. She speaks English and says 'ego' instead of 'I' — which sounds more egotistic.* I was saying that Lucifer works in the ego — for instance if we wallow in self-reproach and imagine that we ought to be better than anyone else. Is that right?

Erik: Yes. But the I is a precondition for our self-directed evolution.

Hilke: Many people have often thought that they would start meditating, but then find that they didn't actually do it. Can you say anything about the I in relation to meditation?

Erik: The I determines that we will meditate but Lucifer is the one who prevents us doing so.

Hilke: But what has happened when we finally succeed in meditating regularly?

Erik: Christ has helped in the I.

Hilke: For someone who has not got so far yet, what would you advise for finding this help from Christ?

Erik: Not to have excessive expectations of oneself but to

---

*The 'I' referred to here is the highest member of the human being, his core spiritual individuality. The word 'ego' can have the same meaning, but is also tinged with other meanings, as for example in psychoanalytic views of the human being.

be modest and just sit down regularly on one's chair and wait for Christ.

Hilke: Is it the I, or the ego, or what is it that succeeds in letting us remove ourselves from all habits and obligations in order to be able to do this regularly?

Erik: The I must do this itself. For this period of time it must free itself from Lucifer. Otherwise the I is never free of Lucifer. But when we love, or meditate, or do something selfless, then Christ works in us instead of Lucifer.

Hilke: How beautifully you put this!

This has been a long conversation, and I'd just like to know if there's anything more you'd like to say on this theme.

Erik: There is, but we'll do it another time.

Twenty-second conversation

I wanted to bear witness to Christ

Hilke: In your wonderful comments on Christ there is something you once wrote which I do not fully understand. You said that you were unable to properly develop your nervous system before birth. Why was this?

Erik: This is because Ahriman prevented me from doing so.

Hilke: How could he gain the power to prevent you?

Erik: I was so devastated by my experiences during the Hitler period that I could not get past him. And therefore I could not connect with the powers that would have helped me. And so I became autistic.

Hilke: Do you know why the nervous system was affected specifically?

Erik: No, but everything else functions OK. It was my nervous system that Ahriman was able to affect.

Hilke: Why do you think Ahriman wished to ruin your nervous system in such a dire way?

Erik: So that I could not bear witness to Christ. If I had been healthy I would have become a priest and would have given sermons on Christ. Now I am unable to preach, but I can still write about Christ. I am not alone in this destiny, but many people with autism share it too. We were so devastated by Ahriman through experiencing his frightful power during the Hitler period. In future we will once again become proper human beings.

Hilke: That is a great comfort to me, and perhaps also for others who will read it. Do others with autism also know this? And may there also be a positive aspect to the great suffering you endure in this present life, in which you are unable to speak and are regarded as completely unintelligent?

Erik: All those with autism who can't speak know this. The benefit is that we learn patience, consideration and love through coming so close to Christ.

Ahriman has no more power over us

Hilke: How is it now with Ahriman's power over you?

Erik: Ahriman has no more power over us.

Hilke: In response to the question about how we can help children with autism you once stressed that we ordinary people and parents should give them love above all. Can you say any more about this?

Erik: Love is the most important thing, but FC is also important. It helps us enter into conversation with you, and helps stop us despairing. But you have to know also that we can always help you with your worries if we can write with you.

Hilke: Yes, Erik, you can help us with our worries like no ordinary person! And can give us the very best advice for our own self-development. Who would have believed this before we experienced it! Sadly there is so much you can't do as well as we can, but at the same time you have advanced much further than we ordinary folk!

Erik: We get help from our spiritual advisors and directly from Christ.

Hilke: And you have already described how one can come closer to Christ.

Erik: Yes, that's what I want to show you in these conversations.

Hilke: Thanks, dear Erik, for this conversation, and for all that you have confided to me. Would you like to write any more, or should we go to bed now?

Erik: We can go to bed.

Twenty-third conversation

Hilke's childhood

Erik: I want to write about Hilke's childhood. Hilke's mother wanted her very much but she herself had not been loved and so she could not love her child. But she did everything, and maltreated her child so that it would become 'cominacked'.

Hilke: Erik, what does 'cominacked' mean?

Erik: It means being able to endure both cold and warmth and being toughened up.

Hilke: Now I understand, and that's true.

Erik: It was a hard time for you. You learned not to cry, for otherwise you'd be sent to the really horrible attic because your daddy was ill and could not bear you crying. Now you can cry whenever you like. You do this for example when you think about the tormentors and torturers of the Hitler period. They lost their divine 'coer'.

Hilke: What is 'coer'?

Erik: That is their divine core or essence. It is their subconscious, fairly painful memory that they were once inhumane tormentors.

A former incarnation of Hilke's

Hilke also lived such a life, though under quite different circumstances from the Nazi period. But you overcame this and can now stand by difficult people who have lost their divine core. They can retrieve it through Christ if someone prays for them. You do so every day. Then they can come back to Christ and learn to love. This is the most important thing you do in your life.

Hilke: Ah, I had no idea!

Erik: You have always wanted to help capable people to understand colossal 'vugurs'.

Hilke: Now there's another word I don't know – what are 'vugurs'?

Erik: They are Hitler's criminals. You had at least one former life when you were locked up for being a threefold murderer. You wanted to revenge yourself on those who had trusted in your opponent and had helped him gather his mounted troops. They sought out your friends and killed them. This was in the tenth century. They did not wish to kill you but just torture you. At that point they were the tormentors, but then you got free and revenged yourself, and tortured them still worse than they did you. Since then you no longer wish to revenge yourself but just be conciliatory. Now you are even able to pray for torturers.

Hilke: Thank you, dear Erik, for this dreadful and enlightening account! Should this conversation be included with the ones about Christ?

Erik: Yes. This is important for understanding your commitment to the tormentors.

Twenty-fourth conversation

Hilke: Hello Erik, you have written that we still need a further conversation relating to Christ, something about your brothers as I understand it.

Erik: All three of us wanted to come to you two because you wanted to have us with our autism. You were well prepared for receiving us and giving us faith that we are proper human beings.

Hilke: Yes, the remarkable thing is that while still very young I completed part of a curative education training, and at the time imagined that I would have known what to do if I myself gave birth to a disabled child. With Andreas I wasn't yet able to manage this, but then I got a second chance with you and Markus. I was never unhappy about having three children with autism, and this seems mysterious when one meets other mothers with just one 'severely disabled' child.

Arrangements agreed in heaven

Erik: In your last life you yourself were severely disabled, and received a great deal of love. And so you wanted to help other disabled children.

Hilke: Yes, that could explain a thing or two.

Erik: Not only were you unable to speak, you could not even walk and had to be carried. This was why you weren't sad.

Hilke: But I don't remember this.

Erik: It was in heaven that we agreed that we should come to you.

Hilke: But I wasn't in heaven between the Hitler period and your birth.

Erik: You were asleep when we agreed this, but awake in heaven, and did not remember when you awoke.

Hilke: This is so interesting Erik!

Erik: Markus and Andreas also met death through Hitler.

Hilke: And both of them now write things with the aid of FC that can help us normal folk to advance further in our spiritual development.

Erik: That is true. They can do so because Christ teaches them.

Hilke: As he taught you?

Erik: Yes, I learn from Christ what you need to know. And others also ask me and I can ask Christ for help and tell them what Christ has said.

Hilke: Yes, and they are so grateful for your mediation!

Erik: Andreas and Markus can also do this. This is our contribution to evolution. We can make this contribution because we get so much help from you [plural].

Hilke: I wonder if others who write with FC have the same capacity. Some of them show that they can certainly advise us in an entirely selfless and responsible way.

Erik: This is true, but not all of them can. Those who can take their lead from Christ do so, but the others write what they themselves think, and it is not good to heed this. They may take their lead from Christ too sometimes, but then you will not be sure what to believe. You can gladly ask me if you are not sure.

Hilke: Thank you Erik for your explanation and your offer. Is there anything more you'd like to write on this theme?

Erik: No, but you must include this under our conversations on Christ — as the last of the conversations between us two.

An FC conversation between Martin and Hilke

Martin, a young adult man with autism, who is unable to speak a word, asked me (through FC) to tell him about the time of Hitler, and above all about the concentration camps. I told him briefly about the death camps such as Auschwitz and the labour camps like Dachau, where the prisoners were communists, homosexuals, various denominations of Christians, as well as ordinary people who had voiced their doubts about Hitler and his views. To be sent there it was enough to have asked, for instance, where all the vanished Jews had gone. I had visited Dachau after the war with my class, and a former inmate had given us a guided tour. Now I told Martin the little I could remember of what he had told us at the time.

Then he wrote on the alphabet board: 'Be glad you don't know more about the concentrations camps.' He followed this up by referring to 'the magnificent thing you did on Sunday'. This was when I had, for the first time, taken Erik's advice about how to do something for those who had been ensnared into torturing others to death. He had suggested I let them be present at the Act of Consecration, and I had tried to do this that Sunday morning. Throughout the service I had been unable to hold back my tears.

We have one of them amongst us

Now I asked Martin whether he knew any of the former tormentors, and he wrote: 'We have one of them amongst us.' Then I considered for a few days the possibility that he himself might have been one of them. On a previous occasion he had written that he had not wanted to be able to speak in this life because he did not wish to do things people had been compelled to do during the Hitler period. But of course he would no longer have had to.

When we wrote again together a few days later, Martin immediately took up this this theme again.

The most satanic invention

Martin: You guessed right, I was a tormentor during the Second World War. It was not easy for me to say this. I was employed as a prison guard at the huge Dachau concentration camp, near Munich. It was there I saw what happened to prisoners. With each prisoner it was my 'delightful' task to oversee them and direct them to the labour they were supposed to do. They had to work until they keeled over, dead; and then we had to procure new prisoners to continue the hard labour. It was a tough task for decent people to ensure they worked hard and did not slack. This wasn't easy, but you had to do it if you wanted to escape the same fate. It was so indescribably awful that one couldn't get away from it. It was the most Jesuitically terrible way to make people obey. No one can imagine how frightful this was. It can't be described. It was the most satanic invention anyone could have thought of.

Hilke: You once told me that when you were in heaven you helped ensure that after the end of the war the peace would be one in which each individual, in collaboration with others, could embark on better self-development. You must therefore have died before the end of the war.

Martin: I died of malaria towards the end of the war. People were injected with it because the doctors wanted to develop a malaria vaccine, and so we caught it too. It wasn't easy that the French could then say all died of malaria, when in reality we died of hunger and frost. That was what took most people's lives, but malaria took the rest. That was the last straw, but we were all starving. You can't imagine how appalling this was. It is impossible to imagine that such a thing could happen.

Hilke: Were you allowed to live outside the camp?

Martin: I never got out of the camp, but had to live with the other prisoners. It was terrible never to see one's friends.

Hilke: And if you had withdrawn from all this, for instance by taking your own life, it would presumably have made little difference since someone else would have taken your place, and nothing would have improved for the prisoners.

Martin: You're right. If you didn't do it, someone else would do it instead in just as terrible a way. I so much wanted to discuss this with you so that someone who is now involved in my present peaceful work also knows what I once did. You can cope with this because you have prayed for tormentors. You have even prayed for people who intentionally tortured others to death. I did not have to do that. Fortunately I escaped that. It was fortunate that I did, for those who did this were unable to find their way to Christ.

After death it was enormously painful

Hilke: How was it for the tormentors after death?

Martin: You're right, it was worst for them after death. They had to suffer everything that those whom they sent violently to the grave had suffered. After death it was still worse for all of us who had done anything like this. It was enormously painful. No one can imagine it. It was the most terrible thing that so many had suffered so much through being told they must work ever harder, when they already couldn't manage it any more. It was so painful to have to experience this oneself — almost unendurable. Then I did not wish to be reborn with any capacity to be forced to do such a thing again. This is the reason I can't speak now. I told you that once before, but you did not as yet know the background to it. You can be quite sure that I can never do such a thing again. I would rather take my own life.

Hilke: But if you had taken your life, someone else would have been forced to do your work and endure your sufferings.

Martin: It's true that another would then have had to do the same thing if I had taken my life. This person has not had to encumber himself with guilt, and that may be some comfort to me. My conviction about Christianity was in fact strengthened by these really terrible experiences. That may be the deeper purpose of all of this. What I experienced was the basis of my capacity to inspire others now to participate in anthroposophy. It was necessary for me to have these experiences. They helped me see better how important anthroposophy is today so that such a thing cannot be repeated. It may well have been a destined thing that I had to experience this.

Hilke: Is it not tempting to torment others when one is in such a desperate and tormented situation oneself?

Martin: You're right, it was a temptation to torment people intentionally, but I was able to resist this temptation. It was a great temptation, and it was not easy to resist it.

Hilke: How was it after death for those who died of hunger, cold and exhaustion?

Martin: Those who died of exhaustion, hunger and cold met with care from Christ and their angel after death, but they did not wish to be born again. But Christ encouraged them to be reborn. He now helps them to have faith in humanity's progress, in the good years that will come after Ahriman has been on earth. This will be soon, and then all will improve if Ahriman can be overcome. Let us hope that this succeeds. We must really hope so, for otherwise the whole of humanity will be done for, apart from a few who can now learn to meditate on the Foundation Stone. This will only be a few, but it means we can rebuild the world anew. We can do this if we do not lose the Foundation Stone. You have no idea how important it is that you meditate on the Foundation Stone each day. This is the most important thing you can do in life, the most important thing of all. You have no idea how important this is for us all, but you shouldn't fall asleep again afterwards. (*This had happened to me that morning.*)

Inviting former torturers to the Act of Consecration

Hilke: But how is it after death for those who intentionally tortured others?

Martin: Those who succumbed to the temptation to torture others intentionally, undergo unimaginable sufferings after death. They descend to the lowest depths of hell where there is no peace, and they cannot get out again. You can invite them again to the Act of Consecration. There they can learn things about Christ they cannot otherwise learn. No one else has so far done this for them. But you were able to because you had done something similar in a past life, in organizing who could be used to execute great building works in ancient Egypt. You tortured those who did not wish to take part, until they agreed. But they did not die from it. Those who worked in the concentration camps have still greater guilt, and they are the ones who now need help. You simply don't know how much they wish to be involved in rebuilding a new, better society. That is their greatest wish. They really want to do this. It is their great hope. They really want to be able to do this but first they must find their way to Christ — and they can do so if we help them to participate in the Act of Consecration of Man.

That was all for today.

4   Questions to Erik and Martin

by Wolfgang Weihrauch

Originally we had agreed that I would put many further questions in relation to the previous discussions, and also on other matters. The dialogue below is the beginning of this, picking up on various themes in the discussions about Christ. Further answers were not forthcoming however. Due to the brevity of some answers in these discussions, as well as some inconsistencies and the difficulty of describing supersensible visions, especially via FC, many questions arose and many still remain unresolved. The answers below from Erik—mediated by Hilke Osika—were based on written questions I had sent in. A few days later Martin also added a few responses, which we have integrated at the relevant places in the text below. Martin, rather than Erik, responded to other questions. This dialogue took place at New Year 2010/2011.

The worst time since the beginning of Creation

Wolfgang Weihrauch: Can you say in a little more detail how the crimes of the Nazi era appeared from the spiritual world?

Martin: During the war things were very grave in the world of spirit. At the time we saw no light in the world, for we had nothing to hope for, and this created the basis for a terrible abyss in the spiritual world; it was terrible because we were unable to see any end to the misery.

It was a fortunate destiny that Hilke came to us, and we can hope to be able to continue with worthwhile tasks in our next life. That wasn't what you asked, but it must be said that for us the most important thing is to be able to communicate with all of you. You do not know this, but that is the new, innovative way for communicating with those who cannot speak. But we need facilitators for this, people who meditate regularly, otherwise they cannot reach us in the place where our consciousness is.

Now let's continue with the new questions. It was an important question you asked. For the world of spirit this was the worst time since the beginning of Creation. It was a terrible insight for the angels that there are powers that can destroy human sensibility, soul and heart to such a degree. It was no longer possible for them to intervene.

W.W.: What ghetto did you liberate Jews from?

Erik: That was the ghetto in Hamburg.

Martin (later): It wasn't a ghetto, but they lived together there.

W.W.: Where or how did you hide the Jews?

Erik: I hid them in the cellar and in the neighbour's cellar. A friend of ours lived there. We had a great deal of contact, and we read the Class Lessons, the esoteric lessons of the School of Spiritual Science.* My friend was also seized and tortured to death.

W.W.: Can you say how many Jews you freed, and how you were betrayed and arrested?

Erik: I was able to free three Jews who then lived in our cellar, and another three who lived with the neighbour. We all read the Class Lessons together, for they were all anthroposophists.

W.W.: Can you say any more about your time in the concentration camp?

Erik: We were very hungry and tired. We had to work very hard, and were treated in an extremely derogatory and inhumane way.

Martin (later): Erik's account was very moderate—he

---

*Founded by Rudolf Steiner in 1923. The 'Class' refers to the first, or initial, stage of the School.

makes it sound almost pleasant. In reality it was a great deal harder. No one can describe it. It was hell on earth, so boundlessly inhuman that one can scarcely imagine it today. It was so terrible that we never wanted to have another life here again on earth.

The school of Christ

W.W.: You say that before birth you attended the school of Christ. How exactly should I picture this? How were you taught? What did he teach?

Erik: We were all in great despair and did not wish to be born again. But Christ showed us that we could go to our tormentors and forgive them, so that they would not land in hell. And we did this.

Martin (later): That was a good answer, and I agree wholeheartedly with it. That was the best school we could go to after the concentration camp, for otherwise we would not have been born again. We would have remained in the world of spirit and would not have evolved further. And that would have been terrible.

W.W.: Can only those who have gone through hell in this life attend this school of Christ? That sounds somewhat unjust, even cruel.

Erik: All can attend this school, but Christ actually brought us there. The others have to seek it themselves.

W.W.: What exactly do you mean by hell, with being imprisoned in hell? Presumably this was after the life before last? Is this the consequence of a life of bad deeds?

Erik: Hell is a place in the spiritual world. There Ahriman prepares people to serve him on earth. I had done these bad deeds and came there. But a good person prayed for me, and so I came to know Christ, and wished to follow him.

W.W.: Can you say anything about this person who prayed for you so that you could find a connection to Christ? Did this happen in the incarnation before last when you did bad deeds? Did this person pray for you nevertheless so that you gained a relationship with Christ?

Erik: He was a relative who prayed for me after I died, for hell is in the spiritual world.

W.W.: What is hell exactly? What realm of the spiritual world is this?

Erik: It is in the lowest part of the spiritual world. Here one is together with other wretches who only have destructive things in mind for human beings. I was there because of, well, sermons, which I held quite a long time ago.

Hilke: What was so wrong about your sermons?

Erik: I preached that people could receive mercy for their sins if they went to a good man and asked him to come to me and give me money.

W.W.: In the seventh discussion it sounds as if one cannot work one's way out of hell during the period between death and a new birth, and that one could be lost to humanity if one did not evolve. Human evolution or development can only relate to the period when we are incarnated, for how can we evolve in the period between death and a new birth?

Erik: Certainly one can evolve in a great many ways between death and a new birth — for instance through gaining new insights, and new, capable teachers who teach one to advance in one's development. It was possible for me to develop through the person who prayed for me; but one can also pray for people whom one does not know.

W.W.: You mentioned 'crass I-egotists'. Can you describe them in more detail? What kind of people are they? When did they live and what did they do? Why can't they be born again? Doesn't karma compensate for every egotistic omission? I thought that every human being had roughly the whole of earthly evolution to develop in, and thus also in future. Is this not the case?

Erik: These are crass egotists who think of nothing other than themselves. Every person has time to evolve, but he has to make efforts too, and not just think of himself. Otherwise he can't get to heaven, and then he can't be born again either. (*It later turned out that 'heaven' is the earth's future, 'Jupiter', spiritual stage – W.W.*)

Hilke: Does such a person end up in hell, or does he go somewhere quite different?

Erik: He enters the most unpleasant hell that lies outside of heaven and earth. There he stays for long ages until God calls him again, to become a being with the animals who then become humans. But then he becomes a strange human being who does not want to participate, and tries to harm other beings.

W.W.: Who created the human I? Was this Christ?

Martin: It was the Father and not Christ, but we need Christ in order to retain and develop our I. Perhaps we can even help Christ in this process if we ourselves go to God and ask him to help us. God helps us when we ask him, but for this we must pray the Lord's Prayer. This is the best prayer we have. Later we receive help from the Holy Spirit when we can remember, in our next life, that we prayed to be able to develop our I towards selflessness. In our next life we will be able to remember this life if we have regularly prayed the Lord's Prayer. But we do not have a great deal of time left. My angel tells me that Ahriman will soon come, and it will then become much harder. Alongside this task we also have that of acquiring knowledge and, if possible, of attending The Christian Community's Act of Consecration. Then we can participate in current evolution.

The task of the Cathars

W.W.: What purpose and tasks did the Cathars have?

Erik: Their task was to come to a Christianity of the heart. They succeeded in this, and now this Christianity exists, and is accessible to all of us.

W.W.: What occurred spiritually as a result of the widespread extermination of the Cathars?

Erik: The spiritual repercussions were that these souls could not immediately return to the earth, and have waited until now. Some of them were able to come sooner, but most of them were fear-struck. But now the whole of earthly evolution is involved, and all wish to help.

W.W.: What guilt did the Catholic Church incur because of this?

Erik: That's a difficult question, for only a few popes did this rather than the whole Church. After death, these popes recognized their errors, and can now work alongside the former Cathars.

Sorath

W.W.: Was Hitler a human being?

Martin: He was a human being like us, but after he was poisoned by gas he was no longer so clear in the head.

W.W.: Erik, you seem to see Ahriman as the great adversary who wishes to destroy all humanity. I don't believe this is correct. Ahriman wants to cut humanity off from the past and from the spiritual world, and make the earth together with human beings into one great machine. This does not fit with eradicating humanity altogether. Am I right?

Martin: It isn't Ahriman but Sorath who wished to eradicate humanity. Hitler obeyed Sorath, above all when his plans to conquer Europe went awry. Sorath gained power over him because he did not wish to give up—this was why Sorath entered the war. Hitler could not see this at the time, but others who no longer had access to him could, people who were no longer able to discuss anything with him. Things could not have been worse than Sorath made them.

W.W.: Erik, what is your view of what you saw as Ahriman? Perhaps Sorath—also a strong ahrimanic being, god of black magic, the beast 666? Or even the Asuras, beings who seek to destroy the human I and originate in a quite different stream of cosmic evolution?

Martin: It is Sorath who originates in a quite different cosmic evolutionary process, not the Asuras. They derive from our earth's Saturn stage. They could not gain access to Hitler, for he did not wish to eradicate the human I—which is what the Asuras desire.

W.W.: Can you say anything about Sorath?

Martin: Sorath is not really a being called Sorath, but is nameless since he was not created by the Word.

W.W.: Can you say anything about the Asuras?

Martin: The Asuras first arose on Saturn, but then were unable to evolve as human beings. They stayed at an earlier stage. Some of these beings turned bad and now try to influence human beings so that they cannot feel good in their bodies, and distance themselves from their further development. Then the Asuras can influence these people in such a way that they become evil beings who in future can become enemies of humanity through their 'human' capacities.

Not seeing the whole panorama of the world of spirit

W.W.: What does it mean that Ahriman or another adversary structured your nervous system in a disabled way? Why exactly? And how does he do this? What makes this possible—some human lapse or something else?

Erik: He can prevent me from seeing the whole panorama of the world of spirit which I need to see to build up my new body. These are all zodiac signs. I could not see the sign of Scorpion, which is Ahriman's sign. He hid it from me so that I should not bear witness to Christ. He was able to do this because I was so afraid of him, and did not manage to pass by him.

We must forgive all human beings

W.W.: Why should one not blame a torturer but instead see him as a victim? He is guilty surely! He could have refused — unless he was really, directly forced to engage in torture, there and then.

Erik: I did not say they have no guilt but that one should forgive them. In the Lord's Prayer we ask that our trespasses be forgiven as we forgive them who trespass against us.

Martin (later): God cannot forgive if we do not ask this. No one can understand this, we just have to accept it is so. We can forgive but we don't always want to. If someone does not forgive me my sin, God cannot forgive me either. It is tragic, but this is how it is. Christ wants us to forgive each other, but we ourselves are the ones who must do this. Otherwise God will also not forgive those who do not wish to forgive the Nazi perpetrators. We all have to understand this for otherwise we get stuck with the ancient Yahveh principle of an eye for an eye, a tooth for a tooth. It would be terrible if this principle ultimately prevailed. What we have done we must compensate for karmically; but if the other can forgive us, then no residue remains to bind us to the earth and prevent us entering the New Jerusalem.

W.W.: In the discussions it sometimes sounds as if you wished to take the burden of guilt away from all the torturers. Surely this is impossible! Then one can simply pass all responsibility to Hitler, or adversary powers. But this is not the case. Every adult human being is responsible for his actions, and therefore more or less culpable. Isn't that right?

Erik: It is self-evident that the tormentors are culpable. But we can never advance in our evolution if we are unable to forgive.

W.W.: It sounds as though someone tortured to death by the Nazis, who is unable to forgive his persecutors, might no longer be able to be reborn. Such a world view is not Christian, but diabolical and unjust. How can someone think straight under torture? How can one ask him to forgive his torturers at this moment? Please can you help me here?

Erik: I did not mean that one has to forgive one's torturers at this moment, but at some point. Of course one cannot think straight while being tortured. But later, in the spiritual world, we can decide either to forgive or take revenge. If one decides on revenge, one goes to Ahriman and joins his hosts — and then one no longer wishes to be reborn. If one can forgive, Christ helps us to be born again.

Martin (later): We cannot know what someone in such a situation can or cannot do; but we can all understand that we must forgive if we have prayed the Lord's Prayer. This is the greatest Christian message along with the one that we should love all people, and also all creatures. Everyone can know this and practise forgiveness; also those who aren't Christians. God sees this in a different way, but we must forgive all human beings if the earth is to continue, and we with it.

This is hard to understand. It is possible for human beings to do this. A longer view shows that it is the only way forward for us if the earth is to survive. God teaches us this if we ask him.

W.W.: Do you mean that forgiveness should slowly grow in life after death?

Erik: Yes. This can take a short or a long time. You can get help in forgiving from Christian people on earth who pray for you, or from people in the spiritual world.

Grateful to Ahriman?

W.W.: How can it be that you see yourselves as messengers of Christ, or wished to be so before being born, although you are unable to speak and can only speak through Ahriman's help — via a PC? Isn't this contradictory?

Erik: We can also pray for you. But when we write on the alphabet board we don't need Ahriman.

W.W.: So should one *also* be grateful to Ahriman?

Erik: One can be grateful for everything that Ahriman makes easier for us.

I'd like to thank you for these questions which clarify what I wanted to say in my 'Thoughts of an autistic person about Christ'.

5 How can one perceive the elemental beings?

by Andreas and Hilke Osika

Andreas Osika, born 1959, lived in good curative homes from the age of 8. He could not come home (too strong and tempestuous) until he started communicating with FC in 2005, which enables him to discuss things and be calmer when there are difficulties. A Rembrandt enthusiast, with his mother he has visited over 100 original paintings by this master in Europe. Somewhat tiring for his mother, but very inspiring.

FIRST BOOK

Introduction

Andreas: This is a book about how one can help natural beings to get a real chance, an honest chance to guide our work again in an upright way. That is necessary, for otherwise a new ice age will soon arrive. Ice ages will come when other powers get the upper hand, the so-called Mosospa. This means impersonal powers that desire to steal the good future of the earth for themselves.

There was once a great, external eruption when the Mosospa had to withdraw, but now they are trying to come back and conquer the earth. But if we succeed in helping the good nature spirits to save the earth, then evolution can continue. Otherwise my good nature spirits will depart for the moon, because we do not wish to care for them. Then we will no longer be able to have food on the earth. But if we wish to collaborate with them, we can create a paradise on earth, as it was before Lucifer found his way in.

Only a few people can see the elemental beings today. One really has to search hard to find anyone who can. But we people with autism often can. In my experience we can see them when we are attentive to what we feel when we look at a flower. We can sense whether we get a calm feeling or some other feeling—not just a generalized sense but a good or bad feeling: a full, astute feeling or another kind of I-imbued, delineated feeling. Here the elemental being is using the Christ power in the ether. At other times one can get more a sense of caraway fragrance when encountering the flower spirit. This is a charismatic being in the flower that wishes to come to our aid.

But we have to approach the flower and show it our esteem before the nature spirit gives us help. Its help involves allowing us to participate in its knowledge of this flower. After all, we can't know just when a flower will blossom—in spring sometime no doubt, but not exactly when. But if we can speak with it, it will blossom when we wish. We can ask it to flower on a certain day—for a celebration perhaps. We can also ask the flower to wait a few days until the birthday or festival. Then the flower will gladly wait. Normally we cannot know when a flower will blossom, but by this means we can determine it.

In the same way we can determine when it will bear fruit. Here again we can ask the plant to wait or to speed up a little. But to do so we must show it our love and esteem. You can't expect it to do what you wish without giving it something. We also need to know that it does not want us to determine its growth arbitrarily, but wishes us to discuss why we wish it to delay or hasten its processes. Then we will get a reply from the flower, as to whether it is possible to change the time of flowering or fruiting.

Hilke: This seems excellent advice, dear Andreas. How can you know something like this which we normal folk without autism usually cannot know?

Andreas: We know this because we can speak with the

flowers and hear their replies. That is the benefit of autism — that we experience nature as ensouled and can speak with nature beings. We can't speak with human beings, but we can speak with elemental beings.

Christ wants us to come to him through the flowers. We do this by enduring to look at them and by giving them our love and admiration. We don't want to come too late to Christ again, as many of us did when he trod the earth. It was a shame that we didn't acknowledge his greatness at the right time. But now we can be there at the due time, seeing him in nature and having a direct experience of the great love that streams from him. This love is greater than anything we can otherwise experience.

My so-called autism means that I cannot say this to anyone. This is why I want to write this book. My aim is to be able to describe Christ so well that everyone can learn to see Christ in the plant realm. This will be a book about the nature beings and Christ in the plant world.

One can also see Christ with one's heart if one does not earnestly wish to see him directly, but instead just loves the flowers and trees, the bushes, berries, insects and birds, midges and all other creatures. One can long rejoice at these living entities. We can observe them for a long time, with wonder, but not pick the flowers for then they die and we cannot take responsibility for their death. We can pick some of them, but then must put them in a vase and admire them with special wonder. Otherwise they will be greatly disappointed. It is important for you to know this, for you shouldn't pick them at all unless someone is going to come and admire them.

My first love was a rose that I was once given for my birthday. I loved it until it faded and died. Since then I have always loved roses. But I have never been given one again. Now you know this and you can give me a red rose again some time, for roses are an emblem of love. All lovers know this and it is true. But we cannot know whether

Christ is in the rose before we see it. This depends on whether the zodiac is [properly] involved as it grows.

It is important which zodiac sign is in the sky. This means, for instance, that Venus may enter the sign of the Crab when the plant germinates. This is a constellation that favours flowering; and when Saturn enters the sign of the Virgin [Virgo], fruit formation is enhanced.

Hilke: How do you know this?

Andreas: I know this from my angel. Recently you were reading about nature beings. They want me to write about some of them that exist here in Sweden. They are quite different from those in Germany, more like the ones in Switzerland. They can't approach people so easily. But at the same time they would like us to make contact with them. One can do so by establishing a connection with decent trees, by feeling our way into them and sensing their qualities. Nature beings do not want us to think about them but just to sense their qualities in a feeling way. Then we should dwell in this feeling for a while. Later we can reflect and think on what we have experienced. Beforehand we shouldn't be too expectant about experiencing anything special. It is very important to be completely calm and neutral. It doesn't matter if you don't experience much to begin with; but once you have started you should carry on for otherwise these nature beings become sad and don't want to try approaching a person again.

I remember once when we were in a zoo and saw a pheasant that didn't want to eat anything. But you gave it an apple, and it started eating it. I saw a small elf that told me I should tell you that you are a good person who does not wish to eat pheasants but feed them with good apples. I can still remember this so clearly, as if the elf were still before me.

My younger brothers can also read thoughts, but I think not as well as I can. But they can see the elemental beings, which you ordinary people can't. But you can learn it from us. You can see them when you open yourself to the beauty of a flower, and ask to see its elemental spirit. Then this will be granted. But you have to know that you should praise him for the beauty of what he has made. Otherwise he will no longer wish to show himself. This would be a shame for all the others who wish to see him subsequently.

You can also see them if you go to other flowers and ask to be allowed to see their elemental spirit, and give them a gift. This would a little pre-taster of being able to play a musical instrument. Then they themselves can learn to do it once one has shown them how. You hum a tune, and imagine you're playing it on a violin or flute. And then you show them how to play the tune on the instrument – in thought only, without an actual instrument. Then the nature beings can understand. But you can't see them before you can pray for them. The prayer to the angel of another person is good,* and is also the best prayer for the elemental beings. You just pray it for the elemental being instead of a person. Then you can also pray it for a plant you love. It's easy. Then you first have an intimation of the elemental spirit that belongs to the plant, and after that you can see it.

You did this, didn't you, for a horse chestnut, and now it wants you to do it again so that it recovers. It will if you carry on doing it, praying for it once a week. It is good to do this on a Thursday, the day of Jupiter, to which it wishes to

---

*This verse by Rudolf Steiner is as follows in the English version:

Spirit ever watchful
guardian of your soul,
may your wings bring
my soul's petitioning love
to the human being upon earth
entrusted to your care
so that, united with your power,
my prayer may radiate with help
to the soul whom my love is seeking.

belong. You can pray for all horse chestnuts at the same time on Thursdays. My spiritual advisor suggested this.

How can we help the elemental beings?

We can help them by making more careful use of natural resources, and by being grateful to them. This would be a great help for them. You are grateful, it is true, but there are many others who go into the woods and to the sea, the fields and meadows. It would mean so much to them if we human beings were more grateful for all the beauty they create around us. We cannot imagine how much labour is invested in the least straw-stalk and everything else. We do not know that they do this work out of love for us and the angels.

We should not gather everything to ourselves so acquisitively. My good elemental beings feel so let down by us, and then they lose all desire to produce our food and drink. Then we may have to go hungry and starve to death.
Hilke: If not everyone can learn to be grateful, would it be enough for a certain number to understand this and practise gratitude?
Andreas: It would be sufficient if those who use bio-dynamically grown vegetables would show their grati-tude. At present you are usually mostly very grateful that such food exists, but you are not grateful to the elemental beings that have created it. You can show your gratitude to them by blessing vegetables and fruits before you chop them. You can do this by making the sign of the Cross over them, as sign that you thank Christ in the produce. As you do this, you can think 'Christ in Us', meaning both in the vegetables and in yourself. This is how grandmother used to bless the bread before she cut the first slice. I saw her do this once in Vienna and it made a great impression on me at the time. But you should always do this.

Now I'd like to describe how we can enter into contact with nature beings. We can call on them in our thoughts in the same way as we might call a person. But only in thoughts, so it can't be heard. Then they come immediately. For instance, you can call upon the spirit who will help lead you to the spirit of the plant with which you seek contact. This is easier than you imagine. But you have to take care not to use the wrong name for this small spirit. His name is not pixie or leprechaun, but Gustav.* That's a nickname for him. No one is allowed to know his true name. He's a small dwarf with a dwarf's hat on his head. He's the one who knows about all the woodland beings. But he does not want us humans to call on any elemental at random: he wants to decide whom we may speak with.

He wants us to start talking to the flower beings especially, since this is easiest for beginners. Then come the tree beings and later the higher, so-called spirit beings who take care of larger areas in the woods — for instance a brook or a meadow with many flowers. Then you can advance further and speak with the angel of a landscape.

You can speak with them about their tasks and ask them how their flower is and whether any help is needed in a particular meadow. For instance, you can offer to say a prayer for the elemental being's flower. Such a prayer could be the Lord's Prayer directed to the spirit who cares for the flower, or a prayer for spirit strength for the flower that needs support, or a blessing for the plant to help it thrive.

You can also pray for the capacity to support the plant by allowing your hands to hover over it for a few minutes in blessing. This alarms the evil powers, gives an impetus for

---

*Translator's note: It is not clear whether this is only applicable in Sweden, since elemental beings may well vary somewhat in nature and name depending on specific locality.

them to flee. To do this, hold your hands over the plant for several minutes and ask to give part of your strength through your hands to strengthen the plant. This does the plant a lot of good. If the plants are larger, you can put your hands around the trunk or the bush, likewise giving it some of your strength. This is good for them, and does not diminish your own strength — but increases it through the gratitude of the spirit.

You are already able to help plants in this way — but you did not know this until the azalea that was almost dead gained new life through your hands. Now you know it, and can do it again whenever necessary.

We can also help plants to blossom with a little lovely music. You elaborated the natural scales, and the elemental beings love these. They want to hear humans playing them everywhere. You should pass them around to all the people you know, and then the elementals would rejoice.

Hilke: In what form should I publicize them? It's true I have tuned various instruments to the natural scales, and sometimes we play them on these instruments. I have tuned both wood and slate bars and aluminium bars to these scales; and also stringed instruments. This means that all the overtone and undertone harmonics of a certain tone are present within one and the same octave. This becomes a wonderfully harmonious and vibrant sound (*see box, over*).

Andreas: Maybe one could do this by arranging the chimes so you can dribble a ball over them.

Hilke: Do you mean arranging the chime bars in a ring with a ball in the middle that rolls round and strikes tones from them? Or hanging wooden chime bars and a ball hanging in the middle of them that strikes them when the wind blows? But you'd need a lot of tuned chime bars — about 16 for an octave.

Andreas: It would be good if they were hanging outdoors where something is growing. This strengthens the

What is an overtone or undertone harmonic series?
by Hilke Osika

When a good friend calls us up on the phone we can already tell by his voice who is speaking. Even if we hear a certain tone on a musical instrument that we can't see, we can usually hear by the sound whether this is a wind or a string instrument or a piano. The particular sound of a voice or an instrument depends on the accompanying resonance of so-called overtones. If you blow into a wind instrument with increasing force, you hear ever higher tones in the overtone series. In stringed instruments, this overtone series appears in the so-called flageolet tones, obtained by placing the finger very lightly on a string. These tones are mathematically determined as lying ever close together the higher the tones are.

We never hear these tones in isolation but they compose the particular sound of a voice or of an instrument. A whistle has only a few resonating overtones while a cello has many.

Starting from a particular octave (tone level) these overtones are whole tones. In other words, the first tone in each octave region is a normal whole tone. Then the tone intervals become ever smaller, diminishing to a semi-tone shortly before reaching the octave note. Mathematically this is written as fractions of the Hertz number (vibrations per second) of the base tone, as follows: 8/8, 9/8, 10/8, 11/8, 12/8, 13/8, 14/8, 15/8, 16/8.

In the so-called undertone series, the relationships are reversed. Here the tones are calculated from the upper octave note downwards: 8/8, 8/9, 8/10, 8/11, 8/12, 8/13, 8/14, 8/15, 8/16 of the Hertz number. Here the tone intervals become ever smaller as we descend through the series.

If we now tune all these tones within an octave on an instrument, the effect is strange but not in the least dissonant: very unusual yet extraordinarily alive — like a rushing, splashing mountain stream, as many have described it.

elemental beings, and so they ensure that the plant grows well. You wouldn't need the whole octave. The first five tones of the overtone series and the corresponding tones of the undertone series would be sufficient. That wouldn't be more than nine different tones.

Hilke: I once saw a set of chimes like this, using round wooden bars that struck against each other when the wind blew, without a ball in the middle.

Andreas: Very good. Then all can strike each other. You can suggest this.

Hilke: Do you have any further tips, for instance what type of wood should be used? Or a different material?

Andreas: The (___) company will know best about that. But you have to say that the sounds must be strong and clear and they must be very precisely tuned, to exactly the right frequencies. The base tone should be A.

Hilke: A = 440 Hertz or A = 432 Hertz? Or something else?

Andreas: A = 432 Hertz.[*]

Hilke: Many thanks for that! Is there anything more you would like to write?

Andreas: Gustav wishes to say that you should use chimes made of Canada wood[†] — an especially hard wood. That's all.

Martin: This was the best part of your work with FC — that you can now help the elemental world with chime bars. These will be more important than much else that can be done for the nature spirits. This will be the most important thing that is done for them in Europe. You just have to ensure that your book is translated and includes a CD disc

---

[*] Note by Hilke Osika: From the base tone 432 Hz to the fifth 648 Hz, which must be present, there would be ten tones altogether: 432, 461, 486, 494, 532, 576, 594, 628 and 648 Hertz. Designated by 'o' or 'u' to show whether a tone belongs to the overtone or undertone series, this gives the following sequence: o u o u u o u o u o.

[†] Translator's note: It is not clear what type of tree this refers to.

of the scales. It is extremely important, essential, that the chime bar tones have the right frequencies. If not, the effect will not help but hinder. They must start with the base note A = 432 Hertz and rise up a fifth. It can be an octave higher, too, but not an octave lower.

Other nature beings

Andreas: The nature beings that Erik describes are not the same ones that Andreas sees. They are other ones that cannot help so much because they are 'selao'.

Hilke: What does 'selao' mean?

Andreas: It means independent. Andreas does not wish for help from such elemental beings. They can only help children but not us adults.

Hilke: But Erik's text is, after all, about how to help children; and if these elemental beings, the sylphs, can do this in a good way, we can be grateful to Erik for his advice surely?

Andreas: That's true. But the undines of which he speaks do not use good methods in relation to children, and I don't wish to involve them. They are bad undines, but mine are good. But they do not concern themselves with children. I think this should be written down in a different way, for it might otherwise be misleading for readers. My undines work with plants, and Erik's undines with the water in brooks and rivers. They are quite different types of undines.

Hilke: Your undines are Christian undines, it seems. How is it with the undines in streams and rivers?

Andreas: They vary. Some are Christian while others are not.

Now my book is finished. One can see nature beings everywhere. My book aims to teach friends to see them. My friends are all those who read my book and wish to be able to see the nature beings. My book is finished.

SECOND BOOK

Hilke: Hello Andreas, I'm pleased that you want to write more about the elemental beings and Christ in nature. We need to know more about such things!

Andreas: I'll dive straight in, then we've done it! Bananas are not good food for us, as their elemental beings don't want to help us with our development. But biodynamically grown bananas are very good: their elemental beings are so grateful for this type of cultivation that they do try to help with our development. But we can't always be sure that they are really biodynamically grown. We can be taken in. However, you can tell by looking whether they are bio-dynamic produce, for then they are smaller and taste different. Then you know.

One can tell a lot from the aura of vegetables. Their auras really vary a great deal depending on whether they are grown conventionally or biodynamically. But that's something you don't see. You have to learn to tell the difference. But to do so you'll have to learn to perceive the elemental beings. You can do this by following my advice in the first book. As yet you can't see them, but soon you'll be able to. And then you will also see Christ in nature. He is with the good elemental beings that are present in bio-dynamically grown vegetables and fruit. Organic produce is not as good as biodynamic because these crops do not benefit from the [biodynamic] preparations. But their ele-mental beings are also Christian.

My guardian spirit would like us to write every day for two weeks so that I can finish my book. Now we can write for longer than before,[*] but we have much more to write. My book will eventually be used in biodynamic training in Germany, but it will take a few years before it is printed in Swedish.

---

[*] Less than an hour each week – H.O.

Hilke: Hello Andreas, do you want to write more of your book?

Andreas: Yes. We can't go on being so brazen with the elemental beings as we are at present — for then my good elemental beings will no longer want to be involved in producing vegetables and grains for us. We must learn to thank them whenever we eat, otherwise they will no longer work for us. My good elemental beings don't wish to hope for our thanks and then not receive it. This could signify the end of the earth and of us. One might suppose that they should take responsibility for our food irrespective of this, but we really ought to be more considerate. We cannot demand that they help us if we don't even wish to think of them as our helpers. Surely everyone can understand this.

Why don't all of you want to thank them? You are completely reliant on them and their spiritual help for your food! It is high time that you worked together with them. You can do so without any loss to yourselves. A few people do, certainly, thank them. The others may have to go hungry in their next life because of their ignorance. Those who do not thank the elementals today will go hungry in future.

We can only sow, water and do other work such as weeding. The elementals do the most important things. None of you understand this yet, because you do not see them; but you can still understand that nothing arises by itself. That's not so hard to grasp. The genes are just the architectural blueprint. Then others have to build the house.

Now I am finished for today.

Hilke: Hello Andreas, would you like to write more of your book?

Andreas: My book is growing longer than I thought, for I have so much to say about the elemental beings. We can't grasp how they can make flower petals so colourful and thin and fine, just from water, air and light. Few people can understand this. It seems they must be chemists and artists.

Hilke: At home we have an amaryllis that is just now in full bloom: very fine, large petals of a wonderful, warm, reddish colour. When the sun shines on it, they seem transparent, a luminous red. How can water, air and light be transmuted into such a miraculous form?

Andreas: An excess of life forces lives in these petals. The water spirits transform water into sap, and the air spirits bring forth colour. My angel tells me that you tried to admire the flower. But you do not yet see the elemental beings because you do not wish to bestow borrowed residues of feeling on them, but instead come into direct contact with them. That is good, but you also have to believe that you can see them in their proper glory. As beautiful as the flowers are, these so-called undines and sylphs are far more beautiful. They are still more beautiful. They move the whole time very swiftly and elegantly. You have no idea how different their movement is from that of humans. They are formless and wonderfully beautiful in many different colours and fluctuating forms. It's beyond you to grasp what different kinds of pictures they have of what their task is. They see before them great, living spheres of burgeoning vegetation. They feel best when they can co-create with enough 'zama'.

Hilke: What is 'zama'?

Andreas: Those are 'amama' — all other beings that also help, the little ones who can transform water and air into matter that grows upwards. These are small beings that do not discuss with their angels how to build up the flowers, for that is what the sylphs do. Without them the sylphs could not produce colours. The little ones just make the actual matter for the flower and the undines form this matter, while the sylphs endow the forms with colour.

Hilke: But doesn't the colour consist of chemical substances?

Andreas: It does, but the zama make this substance too,

without it having colour. They make precisely the substance that the sylphs and undines need. This is an extraordinarily intensive collaboration which these beings engage in. They move very swiftly, and apply very powerful, comprehensive energies in order to transform water and air into plant substance. The other elemental beings can then use this substance to configure and form the plant we actually see. But wise spirit beings direct where the substance should go.

That was all for today. You promised to write with me every day until the book is finished. That is good, for then I can remember what I wrote the day before, and this will produce more consistency. But now we have to go or I'll arrive late for supper.

Andreas: It's good that we can write again today. My good elemental beings cannot know that most humans are unable to see them. When I told them this today they couldn't believe it. They see us after all, and my siblings and I can see them. Most people simply ignore them. I am not sure that I see them better than my brothers, but that isn't so important.

My eyes are not so good for seeing things close up, but I have good distance vision. By contrast, I see my good elemental beings extraordinarily well close to me *and* further away. My eyes used to be better, but I can now see the elemental beings better than I used to. They are so happy when we wish to see them, and they now think I will be able to tell you about them. I'm doing so, and wish to carry on until everyone is able to see them.

They have wonderful colours—you've no idea how beautiful. I used not to be able to see them, but I have now learned to.

Andreas: My new book is about my experiences with the elementals. It is very fortunate that you are available to support me every day [in FC writing]. Now I can better recall what I wrote before. I am so glad you're writing with me, for it gives my whole life meaning.

Hilke: ... above all when your books are published and when, hopefully, your whole residential community and all those who can't speak learn to use FC.

Andreas: It is my angel who wishes to use my good knowledge to gain insight into all elemental beings. I would like to help people to learn to see honest beings that they cannot see at present. We need to be able to see them so as to collaborate with them once again. It is really necessary for the future of the earth that we can collaborate with them, for otherwise the earth will become uninhabitable for all humans, animals and plants.

Now we can drive back.

Hilke: Hello Andreas, now you can write more of your book.

Andreas: Now I can say what I wanted to say yesterday, that there may be quite a few of us who can call ourselves seers of elemental beings. You can say this of yourself too, for you saw the lovely, precious, rich 'zgorne'. Those are beings that wish our evolution well. They were present when you were reading Rudolf Steiner's *Philosophy of Freedom* together today. You experienced them with your good feelings, and explained to the other people so beautifully how the amaryllis develops. You understand such things better than the others, but all those with autism understand it. You made a great, strong impression on such beings, who wish to help us with their wise thoughts. All of them there wished you well. My teacher A was also there.

(*Then Andreas wrote several things about the recognition and dissemination of FC.*) We are unable to write if we can't feel our hands; and we don't feel them unless we have someone there who presses them. We want to write with all of you. But this doesn't work if you don't press our hands enough.

Hilke: Would you like to write more of your book now?
Andreas: You're right, we still have so much to write about the elemental beings. They are so keen for you to see them. But soon you'll be able to. If you stand with both feet on the ground, you can't see them; but once you have begun to see them, you can easily develop this capacity. My mother wishes to see them but she doesn't have enough patience to look at flowers for long enough. This will improve with time.

But now we must get down to writing about the beings we can experience with our hearts. These are my good, juvenile children, those who wish to come into the world with new powers. I'm talking about human children. These children will be able to see the elemental beings from the very outset.

Now we can drive back.

Hilke: Hello Andreas, I have brought with me the book 'Master Grey'[*] by [Swedish author] Rebecka Vik. Do you want to look at it now, or take it home with you? Shall we leaf through it here, and look at all the pictures of nature beings?
Andreas: We can look at it now . . .

I'd like to take it home with me. I'd like to meet Rebecka.
Hilke: Do you want to speak to her with the help of FC? And shall I support you?
Andreas: Everyone who gets this book will want to. Only I can see the same beings as she does.
Hilke: Did you recognize any of the beings that she painted while we were looking through the book?
Andreas: I did, but not all of them. To do so I would have to go to the places where they are.
Hilke: She intends to give guided tours to these places, and

---

[*] Not available in English translation.

we can go along too. But in return for payment she also gives private tours.

Andreas: I would like to have a private tour to see these elementals whom I do not yet know. They are mountain beings and those that manifest in woods. But all the beings she depicts are interesting. Especially, expulsive beings that I do not yet know well, that are connected with death and putrefaction. I'd also like to meet other beings that don't occur in homes and gardens. It is so rare for me to get out into wild nature. It is a great gift to come there when one spends one's whole life in an institution. I'd like to meet Rebecka as soon as possible, and it's fine to go for a walk in nature, even if there's snow on the ground.

Hilke: Do you still want to play on the marimba before we drive back?

Andreas: I want to go back now and have lunch.

Hilke: Hello Andreas, now you can write again.

Andreas: You tried to look at the amaryllis for a long time, but you did not see the elemental beings. They were all there but you did not see them. That was such a shame. You must learn to see them with the names of sylphs and undines. My angel says that you made real efforts, but that you can't see them. You can marvel at them but now you must practise perceiving them. As soon as you feel wonder, you'll also be able to have an intimation of their presence. And so you will gradually come to see them. It is so difficult for you clever folk!

Hilke: Now the wonderful, large amaryllis has started to fade. Are the elementals withdrawing?

Andreas: Of course. You can turn instead to the little orchid which is just starting to blossom. It is telling you that you will soon have progressed far enough to see its elemental beings because you can already see how they swirl around it. You need only shut your eyes when you see them swirling, and then they will reveal themselves.

My angel wants me to meet Rebecka soon. You can telephone her right away. Then we can go there tomorrow.

Hilke: ... I have spoken to Rebecka. There's still a lot of snow in the forest, as she describes in her book about the elementals. She says it would be better to go there in a month. She lives in a large industrial region, black with coal dust, but not far from the sea. Would you like to just visit her there? Or what do you think is best?

Andreas: I'd like to visit her where she lives, and speak to her with the help of FC.

Hilke: Would you mind if Erik came too?

Andreas: It's good if he comes. We can both speak to Rebecka. Erik is just as interested in the elemental beings as I am.

Hilke: Then I will try to arrange it as soon as possible. What else would you like to write in your book?

Andreas: The book will soon be finished. But once I have spoken with Rebecka, I can write more.

Andreas: Now I'd like to carry on writing about the elementals. You have now started to see them. The sylphs you saw are the kind that can help plants to blossom. These are quick, rich, minimal beings that move far too fast for one to see them clearly. But they swirl around the flowers.

Hilke: So they are small and very fleeting—but what do you mean by 'rich'?

Andreas: This means that it is easy to see them physically. These are the most 'amandy', coloured mini-sylphs on earth. They can induce all flowers to blossom. The best flower I know is the orchid in your living room. It is so pretty and lovely, has such beautiful colours and fine forms. The large amaryllis has large, powerful blossoms and correspondingly large, powerful sylphs around it. You can sense its sacred beauty. They are wonderfully reverent in their work. You do not know how lofty their angels are. I love the hues and tints of this large amaryllis. You have no idea how much I love this colour. You sense that there are great, holy, mighty beings around it. I can see them with my somewhat refined sense, the same sense with which I can feel my way into your soul. I haven't actually seen them, but I feel what you feel when you look at your plants.

You must water them more often, every other day. The amaryllis has had enough water, and also the orchid, but not the other plants. They are so undemanding that they can be watered this seldom and it's enough for them— because they like you both so much. All these years they have never had fresh earth, but it would do them good.

Hilke: What does 'amandy' mean?

Andreas: It means adorable mini-sylphs.

You can go back to work now, and add this to my work.

Hilke: Hello Andreas, do you want to do more on your book?

Andreas: Gladly. My book should also contain many accounts of other beings. My spiritual teacher would like to ask you if you have observed your orchid today. You should do this every day for a longish period, at least a quarter of an hour. But you have to learn to practise this honestly and peacefully. This exercise is necessary so as to shed the day's thoughts. My teacher can 'noblefile' with you. 'Noblefile' means remembering what one has seen with new eyes. It is not easy to remember what one has seen, but neither is it difficult.

My teacher can see whether you have been talking with your flower or not. You must speak with it so that it can help you with your spiritual vision. It is important to learn to discuss things with your flower in the right way. You can tell it that you wish to see its aura, and learn to sense its need of water and nutrients. You never feed your flowers but sometimes they need a little compost. You do so many other things that are important, but you should not forget your flowers. They want to help you but you should care for them better. Now you can drive home and give them some love and give them my greetings: say I'd like to come to see them. We can go there now. Let's do it. I haven't been to your house for many years, but I know that you have a few plants there still. My teacher says that we should drive there now and visit your orchids. Let's do that right now.

Hilke: Hello Andreas, now I'm looking forward to seeing how your book continues. Yesterday you came home with us for a little while.

Andreas: I discussed what your flat is like with my spiritual teacher. Remarkably disordered, a lot of paper everywhere, dangerous vibrations, a mess. That isn't good for you. Apart from this there are many good elemental beings at home with you, who really like you. But you should tidy up better. Otherwise this will turn into a so-called 'drucal' series of 'submaryas'.

Hilke: Dear Andreas, our flat is much too small for all the papers and books that daddy and I want to produce and store. We have collected so much more than one would be able to do in a residential community like the one you live in. But it's absolutely true that we can tidy things up and arrange them better.

But what is a 'drucal series of submaryas'?

Andreas: It's chaos in your heads when you get older. It would be such a shame for you to get dementia. All your papers will be burned anyway when you die, and whoever comes after you will chuck everything out. You can't take these things to heaven with you.

Your blossoming flowers were so lovely! They say that you are destroying your health by never going for a walk. They heard this from their angels. You don't take time for this. You must. Otherwise you will die of a heart attack. But you really are still very much needed here on earth.

Hilke: Thank you Andreas for encouraging me to take time for my health. Were your flowers as you had imagined?

Andreas: They were exactly as I imagined. But the orchid was even more beautiful. You have the most beautiful orchid I have ever seen.

   Now I'd like to write about my elemental beings. They all want you to see them. They can't wait any longer. You have so many of them in your home that they are really making you shaky. They want you to pray for them. You can do this by praying the Lord's Prayer in your living room. You can pray it quietly, but every day. It's true that you pray it every evening, but you can do it once more in your living room.

Hilke: Yes, we can do this. But in our living room, where the kitchen is too, and where we eat, there is a problem. I have my computer there, and work on it every day; and it disturbs daddy. But I'd rather not have it in the bedroom.

Andreas: As long as you don't work there during the night, you'll be using it in the right way.

Andreas: Now I can continue writing about my elemental beings.

   I would like you to learn to see the elemental beings so as to give them a place in your large heart. But for this you'll need to look at your blossoming plants for much longer than you do at present. I'm sure you'll be able to start seeing them very soon if you take your walks past the horse chestnut tree during the daytime. He'd like to see you again, he's waiting for you. But at the moment there's too much snow on the path. Erik told you, didn't he, that you should pray for the chestnut, and this helped it. But you must go on doing this regularly every Thursday.

Andreas: I would like to meet Rebecka. Her books are so interesting. I have seen quite a lot of what she describes. The more sickly beings are mainly the ones I don't know.

My beings are not as weak and frail as hers, for I only see them in my dreams, on my travels through the great world. Then I can see them in their true forms. But now I can see them as Rebecka does, and I know how they reveal themselves in reality. It is fascinating to compare this with what Rebecka experiences.

But there are other things to discuss, such as varanes, that are so small one scarcely sees them. These beings are not as bulky as Rebecka describes. I feel sure we can all pursue the path recommended by Andreas, to look at a plant for a long time, retain it in our memory, return to our memory pictures and in doing so come to new experiences. This isn't easy, but it is what I recommend.

We cannot come to a proper picture of the elemental beings if we do not wish to work at trying to experience them. It is so important today that we concern ourselves with them, so as to help our earth. The tsunami in Japan (March 2011) was an attempt to show as many people as possible that we are not the lords of the earth but are dependent on clear, minutely responsible elemental spirits. The destruction of the reactor was a catastrophe, but we humans should know that radioactivity is far too danger-ous to be used so widely. We should employ windpower and other alternative energy sources. The nature beings say this. One cannot get any further today without using these alternatives.

I have to tell you that we cannot write any further if you don't take the time to look at your flowers.

Hilke: Hello Andreas, what would you like to say?
Andreas: Can you fetch the instruments tuned to the natural scales?
Hilke: Now we've been improvising on them a little. How do you find it?
Andreas: A little unaccustomed but a great adventure. I can't play on them as you do. You play wonderfully—it

sounds like the music of elemental beings. It's the music of the future, a kind of music we have to develop further. Our present tonal system is much too rigid. But you have found the tonal system of the future. Now I'd like to really ask you to play more.

But you have to look at the orchid before I go on writing my book. You really must, for otherwise you won't believe that I'm seeing something you can't see. You experience dynamic little triangular beings. Those are the sylphs. But you also have to be able to see the undines, which are much rounder in form. The two kinds work together, but you only have a tentative experience of them. You have to see them more clearly before I continue with my book. Now we can drive back.

In a couple of days my book will be finished.

Hilke: Hello Andreas, what would you like to say?
Andreas: You are so keen for me to write more about the elemental beings, but for this all you need is to directly observe the blossoming water beings at home. These water beings also wish to be seen. One sees them in the lower part of the petals, and the sylphs form the other part. That is their collaborative work. But so far you only have a vague inkling of them.

Now we can drive home.

Hilke: Hello Andreas, would you like to write more of your book?
Andreas: There's still a little to write. But you have to learn to put my suggestions into practice every day. At present you only practise every other day. I notice when you practise, and am glad every time; and each time you make progress. It is wonderful that you now experience Etshevit[*] when you see all the undines.

---

[*] See p. 190.

Hilke: But I can't yet speak to him, can I?

Andreas: I'm sure you soon will be able to.

Hilke: You have such an effective way of getting me to practise properly — rather than just losing myself in all the tasks I don't keep up with.

Andreas: Maybe you shouldn't work so much with finances. Others can do that.

Hilke: I don't know who else could make out all our invoices, pay bills, do the accounts etc. But you're right, I should look for someone else.

You also wanted to write about Christ in nature.

Andreas: My task is to teach you to see the elemental beings; then you yourself can discover that Christ is present in nature, wherever elemental beings exist. All elemental beings in nature are Christian, and all of them can tell you about Christ.

Hilke: But if one can see the elemental beings in nature, surely one can also see Christ himself there — or only if the elemental beings tell us of him?

Andreas: Yes, we can always see Christ in nature, and how he properly grasps things we otherwise overlook. There we can see his love for all and everything. But he also wants us to come to him in the night when we're asleep.

Hilke: There's something I have to ask you which I didn't understand: that Christ 'properly grasps' things in nature which we otherwise overlook. What exactly do you mean by this?

Andreas: He makes decisions about how nature should be healed by us human beings using our senses and feelings to nourish and nurture the elemental beings.

Hilke: Hello Andreas, what would you like to say?

Andreas: I would like to go and see Rebecka soon. You must phone her and book a time. It's urgent, for we can help each other.

Today you saw the waterfall, and tried to see the undines

there. There were large water beings present. They look like large elephants tumbling about and spraying the water on each other — you had an inkling of them. However, you were unable to see them as undines, but instead as large water beings that are not undines at all, but have other names that I haven't heard of.

Hilke: I have been wondering whether they stay there in the waterfall in the river Nyköping, under the bridge near the sea, or whether new colossi keep coming there. Your description of them as 'elephants' is really very apt!

Andreas: They may stay there but I don't know. I have never seen this myself. There was never so much water when I went there. You yourself haven't ever seen so much water in the river before. It is so different when you spend so long observing everything that is alive there. Each time you can see more, each time a little more.

Andreas: Now I can write more about the elemental beings. You didn't look at the flowers today, but you will this evening. All elemental beings want to be seen by you and tell you that you are a good seer when you see them. It is good to know that they accept you. They do because you're able to love them. They accept all who love them, and do not accept those who cannot love. Such people have to learn to love, and then they can begin to see the elementals. You must include this in the book.

I can also write about how one can learn to use the harmful effect of my stupid behaviour so that a different, greater Andreas can teach you to converse with the elemental beings. You can ask me and I will ask them. All wish to be asked. This is true of all that is connected with life and living things.

Hilke: That is a fine and important suggestion! But we are also grateful when you yourself write about the realm of life whenever you see that there is something we need to know about it.

Andreas: I can tell you if you ask. Otherwise I may not do so. This is how you can make best use of us. Now we can drive home. Everything in the elemental world is different from how it is in ours. Everything there is completely different from our world.

THIRD BOOK

First questions from Rebecka about the previous books, and Andreas's replies
Rebecka: What kind of beings are 'mosospos'?
Andreas: They are Asuras. They want to take over the world again. They'll be able to if we no longer pray to God. This would be the end of our earth evolution. But we pray to God each day.
Rebecka: What are your dream journeys?
Andreas: Travels in the world of spirit when we are awake while we sleep.
Rebecka: Are these astral journeys?
Andreas: Yes, but we cannot all see the elemental beings while we're asleep. All can see them but only few can remember them when they wake up.

In response to the question as to whether we must approach nature in the company of Christ (as Rebecka thinks) or find Christ in nature (as Andreas thinks), Andreas wrote:
Andreas: It is usually true of Christ that he is in nature, but we human beings have to experience him intrinsically, and also in nature. Nature also needs to know that Christ has risen. The nature spirits know this but not the elemental beings in cultivated plants. They have to be told this by human beings.

24 March 2011
Andreas: You must include this in the book, but not what I wrote about apes.

Hilke: I can't remember you ever writing anything about apes.

Andreas: You've forgotten that in Skansen we saw apes of all kinds using sticks? I wrote that they cannot use our [kind of] thoughts when they do something, but just ape us. They learn from the elemental beings what tools to use. With their atavistic feelings they sense that there is another meaning in progressing so far as to handle tools in a good way. They are animals after all. That can be my next book. I'd like to write it laminately — meaning each time we write together here in the coming period.

29 March 2011

Andreas: Now I'd like to write about animal beings. One does not see them directly, but you can see them if you can see the elemental world. Then one just sees a little of this world, a little more of my good 'papamas'. But I only use my eyes, nothing else, to see them. My 'anamas'. Amanas are like daminas with rather short upper arms. You can see my amanas in various species of animal. The amanas can help animals make their burrows and nests. You can see them best if you get really close up to animal dwellings. They are present there and tell the animals how to use any available materials to build their dwellings. They give animals nuanced advice. But my amanas cannot know whether we human beings will destroy all the dwellings used by animals. But the dams built by beavers cannot be destroyed by humans, and then old ones can be used.

Hilke: But unfortunately people do sometimes destroy the beavers' dams, for instance if they believe that they lead to flooding.

Andreas: All beavers want their dams to be left intact, but they also use old dwellings people have left alone. All beavers like having new dwellings, but people make it hard for them to find good places to build. Not all streams still have trees around them. The beavers need the dams to hide themselves and fish. My amanas can show them good places to build, but they do not know whether humans will accept them building there.

Hilke: Can't we humans help them in any way (apart from not destroying their dwellings)?

Andreas: We can help them by not coming too close to their dwellings and not disturbing them. I myself have never yet seen a beaver dam. It would be nice to see one some time. They can't all have been destroyed.

Human beings don't know what they do when they break up a beaver dwelling. They do not know that they are destroying a place where spirit beings come together with the beavers. These spirit beings have a task in the area where the beavers are. They make it possible to have gladly remaining, honest, beloved, natural amanas in that region. Then all other beings can live there too, and can create a positive atmosphere in this area. Then honest beings can be active everywhere in helping plants to flourish and in making lovely air and good humus. That is actually the beavers' task.

30 March 2011

Hilke: Hello Andreas, it was so interesting to hear what you told me about the beavers yesterday! I am looking forward to hearing what you will say today!

Andreas: I don't want to speak so generally about particular animals but more about their so-called startling anatomy.

Hilke: Yesterday I wasn't sure whether the beings you spoke of are called anamas or amanas.

Andreas: Hilke doesn't want to know whether they're called amanas or anamas, but what I call them. I call them amanas. To find food and building materials for their dwellings, animals need help. The amanas are not their group souls but are spirit beings who help to find what is needed each day.

My spirit tells me that the amanas are good spirits in close proximity to all animals. But we cannot see them because they hide themselves close to animals. They can't know that we are unable to see them anyway. But you could see them if they all showed themselves to you. They do so if you ask. That can be good; otherwise you have to feed birds with apples, and with other things they like. You've no idea how grateful they are for you feeding them throughout the winter. For them, this means that human beings take care of asocial birds that eat up what the familial amanas cannot find in nature during winter. It is then too difficult to find food in nature. But when you feed them they think you are their aman, and they want to thank you by showing you their amanas if you ask them.

Now all those who can see elemental beings can also see the amanas, like Rebecka. I soon want to meet her. But you are going to travel to Finland—where you can't see the amanas because there are other kinds there that don't know you. But when you return you can see them.

It's good that you're going there, since many children there need you, because you teach FC. It is incredibly important for children to learn to write with FC. That's the most important thing in their lives. You have no idea how keen they are to learn to write. For instance, a boy in a wheelchair and a girl who can't speak should learn it. Otherwise they won't make any progress in their spiritual development—they'll be completely unable to incarnate. But with FC they can incarnate so that their brain can develop to the level of the amanas. And then, in their next life, they can use their experiences to help others find their way in life.

This is a great help for these people, for otherwise they will be analogous in spiritual terms to what the animals now seem to be. But for people this is much worse—something like a retrograde step to spiritual so-called machines. This is damage for them, altogether and eternally. And then they can't advance their spiritual development. Damage means catastrophe. But we will be able to help them if we now learn to write with FC. Then we can earth ourselves and help those who have got stuck. It's the most important task we could possibly have in this life.

12 April 2011
Hilke: Hello Andreas, would you like to write more of your book?
Andreas: I can write a little more of my book. It is to be about animals and elementals.

We cannot live on earth without animals — not in order to eat them but because they belong with us. At present we can live without them, but in future ordinary people won't be able to live without their skins when things get a great deal colder on our earth and we no longer have cotton and mineral oil products. My angelos says that I should use my knowledge of threefolding to make life possible for us on earth. Things won't go well for us unless we realize the threefold social organism. We have to learn more about it. This is essential, for otherwise we won't be able to rebuild America once it has been destroyed by our spiritual enemies. In America a grave cultural era is coming. We have to develop corresponding help for America, otherwise others will take possession of my wondrous earth. Now we must learn more about Christ and the threefold social order, otherwise it will be less and less easy to live on our earth.

20 April 2011
Hilke: Hello Andreas, your book is becoming so fine! Do you agree?
Andreas: That's true. We can achieve good things together. Now I'd like to continue with my book on the beloved animals and the elemental beings. My teacher is A who is

now in the spiritual world together with F, who is helping you with FC. A was my teacher in Ireland, and I also went to other teachers who were able to teach me to see nature beings. My teacher did not wish to show me this himself, for I was meant to learn to be a seer without the help of a teacher.

My mother does not wish to see the elemental beings, as otherwise she would practise more. Nevertheless, she is on the right path, for otherwise she would find it too dull to write about this path.

I have been able to see them all my life, because things were so tedious for me as a child. I was able to play with the elemental beings when I was lonely in my room. They told me and each other such amusing things. Next to my bed in Örebro lived a dwarf who made faces and was such fun. Other beings weren't so amusing but wanted to talk about their experiences with other people who did not wish to drink alcohol but just wanted to work with them — like Bert and Marianne. They liked these people very much and wanted me to meet them again. But I never did, and now I want to while they're still alive. I want to go to visit them, right now, for you never know how long they will still be travelling through their life.

10 May 2011
Hilke: Hello Andreas, what would you like to tell me today?
Andreas: You went for a long walk and saw sylphs and undines. That was the first time you really took the time for this. My angel was there and told me that the ancient Druids were also able to see such things. My angel wants you to write down what you experienced as occurring today between the undines and the sylphs. Their collaboration is really unique, and can be exemplary for human collaboration. You experienced this so strongly that it became visible in the latent world of spirit. That is the

world of spirit in all plants, and there it was not known that human beings can experience such a thing. No one has ever experienced this so strongly as you did today. I have not done so either. But now all can know of it, and also experience it. Everyone can read it in my book. But now you must write down what you experienced.

Hilke: I looked at the closed buds of a great many different trees and compared them with those that had already opened a little, and with others that had started to blossom. In the bud-sheaths the zamas create plant substance from water and air, engaging in this with extraordinarily energetic activity; and the undines create green leaves from this substance. But at the same time they wrap and protect the beginning of what the sylphs — sometimes simultaneously — prepare as developing blossoms. The undines provide the sylphs with plant sap, and the sylphs form the blossoms with colour and blossom substance. That is roughly how you and Erik described it to me.

Now I experienced this as a divine collaboration, a uniquely shared and loving creativity. Tell me, how can the water rise through this hard wood and the long twigs of these great trees until it arrives in the furthest buds?

Andreas: It is the undines who suck up the water from the earth through the trunk and branches. Once all the leaves are formed and are transpiring water, this works by itself; but until then it is a great labour for the undines to get the water moving and transport it up into these dried-out twigs. That is their first job after the winter. But they can only do it because Christ helps them with his power of resurrection. This overcomes gravity.

You did not write that you experienced such extraordinary joy and happiness when you saw the sylphs.

Hilke: Yes, I am sure it isn't just the physical blossoms we see when we experience the elementals — without knowing this consciously. The beauty and luminosity of the blossoms is such a joyful sight, isn't it?

Andreas: Your're right, the flowers use their elemental beings to enter our souls and influence us with feelings of various kinds. You have experienced this in the past, but you did not know that the elemental beings are as various as our feelings towards the different flowers.

12 May 2011

Hilke: Hello Andreas, now I have such beautiful experiences in nature, and I owe this to you and your descriptions of the work of the elemental beings!

Andreas: All elemental beings are grateful that Andreas once gained the insight to call upon your good will so that you have learned from me. You could not see them before, but now you can sense them. In a little while longer you will be able to see them at work as well.

17 May 2011

Hilke: Hello Andreas, what would you like to tell me?

Andreas: I want to say that I'd like to continue with the elemental beings. One can't see them physically, but you see them with the heart. My mother is trying hard but her heart is too manic. She doesn't have enough patience to speak with the plants 'millingly'. 'Millingly' means talking to them for a long time. She could do so, but she doesn't take the time. Now the lady wishes to know whether it is she who can see the sylphs, or the sylphs who can see her.

Hilke: This spring I am increasingly overwhelmed by the beauty of the opening flower buds, and I wonder whether this intense experience of beauty comes from the sylphs.

Andreas: One can't experience beauty at all without the sylphs being present. Beautiful pictures are also surrounded by sylphs, if they are the original paintings. You experience these sylphs, and they experience you just as strongly. But they also see you and experience your aura, which they like observing. They also see all your feelings, of compassion and pain, and what you want to do for all of us who cannot speak. They would like to help you with this, help spread understanding of FC amongst all beings in nature, and human beings.

But you have to learn to communicate better with them. Then they can learn to persuade everyone, so that no one will regard FC with distrust.

It would be so important for you to tell everyone that FC is the very best method for us to live a dignified life. All must come to hear this, and you are so good at explaining it. The elemental spirits wish to hear this too. You can tell it to a few trees and bushes, and they can pass the message on to all others. This can help all those involved to understand it. But you also have to tell your fellow human beings who don't yet know about it.

18 May 2011
Hilke: Hello Andreas, what would you like to say?
Andreas: I want to tell you that I don't know what there is to talk about if you don't make any attempt to see the elemental beings. You have to take my word for it that you are going to die soon if you don't go out for walks. Your health is not as good as you believe. You won't live much longer if you don't go out for walks. You can drive back with me now, and then take a walk. My presentations on the elemental world will have to wait until you give some attention to your health. Your health is now the most important thing, but you prefer to write with us. That's very sweet of you, but you mustn't neglect your walks.
Hilke: You have seen our orchids, haven't you? The orchid by the other window, not the one you like so much: its petals are withering now. Am I watering it too much or too little?
Andreas: It needs only a tiny amount of water, you hardly need to water it at all. One dessertspoon of water a week is enough. You haven't watered the others for a while. You must do that today.

19 May 2011

Hilke: Andreas, what would you like to say?

Andreas: My good elemental beings want to thank you for telling them about FC. They did not know that there are people who cannot speak the human language. They were shocked to hear this. But now they understand that they must help to spread the word that we need to be able to write down our thoughts.

Now they can understand us better than they used to, for they know that we are different from other people, and need so much help and understanding. My sylphs definitely wish to help pass this knowledge on to others.

20 May 2011

Hilke: Hello Andreas, I'm looking forward to hearing what you will tell me!

Andreas: I still need to write about Christ—that he will soon come again and will rely on those who now believe in him.

To conclude you can write: My Andreas wishes to entrust these lines to those who cannot yet see the elemental beings but who wish to learn to see them. He would like all you modern people to learn to help them accomplish their work energetically. All of you can help with this. But you can also help each other to go to a good spiritual teacher and learn even more about such things.

All are welcome in paradise, with all your different gifts.

My book is now finished; and my mother will become my very closest and all-understanding friend on earth and in heaven.

6 My Life in Dornach During Rudolf Steiner's Time

by Erik Osika

This was a unique period

I would now like to write about my previous incarnation. My teacher does something wonderful. He teaches me to tell about my former incarnations. This will become a new book for those who would like to know something about the period with Rudolf Steiner. There is not a great deal to write, but it is interesting.

The building site

I was working on the Goetheanum as a builder. I learned to carve and form the walls and ceilings in this new way.

I came to Dornach because I could not find work in Italy. I was an apprentice builder and could learn all sorts of new skills. I worked the whole time. But it was wartime and I had to choose whether to become a soldier or find employment in neutral Switzerland. I was Italian, but I was able to come to Switzerland because my mother was born in Arlesheim, and had later married an Italian. She moved back to Switzerland and took me with her.

We lived in Arlesheim and could see the building site from our window. I was a builder, after all, and I asked whether they could use my help. They said they could, and so I went there to work. We were able to hear Rudolf Steiner's lectures to the workers. They were so interesting that I became a member of the Anthroposophical Society, and also a member of the School of Spiritual Science. My name was Juno Mingreno. To begin with I couldn't speak

German, but I learned it quickly. I became a good colleague of the other people building the first Goetheanum. It's hard to imagine how exciting it all was. This was the best time in all my lives.

I also heard something about the arduous efforts undertaken to try to save Rudolf Steiner's life. People were trying to calm his inner organs with the help of calmative medicines, but he didn't want this. But Ita Wegman insisted. Then he finally agreed, but grew still worse. It was disagreeable for us to hear of this. But we did not immediately come to his [Steiner's] aid, and instead were always sent away again by Ita Wegman. We had Dr Kolisko with us, who later became his doctor, but by then it was too late.

I was only 15 when I arrived in Dornach. But I am glad, now, that I was there.

I cannot remember my father — he had died already. But I remember my paternal grandmother. She was small and fat, very loving and kind. But after we came to Dornach I no longer saw her. My father was a comedian. He could make people laugh, but was himself melancholic. My mother was also small in stature, slender and dainty.

My mother did not wish to stay in Italy when war broke out, but she had nowhere to live in Switzerland. We were able to stay with her parents until we found a flat of our own. My grandparents were good people, and showed me a lot of understanding. They could see why I wanted to work on the Goetheanum.

When I arrived in Dornach, the Goetheanum had not yet been built. The big concrete foundations had already been laid, though, and some wooden pillars — but no walls as yet, or roof. My first job was to fetch the materials for the building — the wood that had been seasoned indoors for some time, at a place close to the building site. There were several of us doing this together, and we had a truck for moving the wood.

My colleagues came from various countries, and we

spoke different languages. But we understood each other through gestures and also had a few words in common.

My mother was pleased that I had work, and a small income. She was not rich, and had left everything behind in Italy. Now she was reliant on help from her relatives, and on the money I earned. It wasn't much but it paid for our food.

During my years in Dornach I was happier than in any other life. My able teacher was my colleague Martin Underberg. There was nothing he couldn't build. He was brilliant at using all the building materials we had there.

Then came the fine work of erecting a wall around the building, so that work could be done on the pillars and the inner wall. This wasn't so easy. I had insufficient know-how. But there were people there who knew how to build an outer wall of this kind, and who taught us. My skills increased and soon I was able to help with building the roof. First it was only provisional, to keep the rain off. Later we built the exterior roof—an artwork involving a great number of roof slates.

One co-worker always had to keep an eye out to ensure that everyone working on the roof had a rope tied around him—otherwise you weren't allowed up on the roof. This precaution meant that no one fell down. But several people nearly did, and ended up hanging by the rope—not for a whole hour but for quite a while until we could haul them up again. My best friend fell off twice, but suffered no injuries.

It was my job to limit the risk of accident: I was entrusted with the task of checking everyone's protective gear. I was the youngest on the site, but was thought to be particularly conscientious.

On the roof, too, I was made responsible for building things in the right order, ensuring that the rood tiles were correctly positioned. I learned this from my friend who was working on the interior at that point.

It was good to have Gredelina with us. That's Edith Maryon. She was always able to convey our wishes to Rudolf Steiner. She was the first woman I loved, but I never told her. I was 19 at the time. I was only 14 when I arrived in Switzerland, in 1914.

Rudolf Steiner's lectures

It was my happy destiny that I came there, but some of the older anthroposophists treated me strangely, saying I was too young to attend Rudolf Steiner's lectures. But Rudolf Steiner wanted me to hear his lectures for the workers. I could not speak much German, but nevertheless understood most of what was said. It was so exciting! The things he spoke of were the most gripping I had ever heard! This was the best time in any of my lives. Rudolf Steiner's clear, articulate voice made it easy to understand him. Every word and every phrase were important, and we were allowed to say what we wanted him to speak about.

It was only at these lectures given by Rudolf Steiner that we all met each other personally. His talks were so interesting.

People no longer know that the best thing about working on the Goetheanum was the way Rudolf Steiner took us so seriously. We were allowed to ask any question we wanted, and he spoke incredibly well in response. On many occasions I wanted to ask a further question, but was too shy. But he sensed my questions and answered them very fully. Nowadays I can scarcely believe that I was actually present to hear these magnificent lectures—but I still remember them so clearly.

My questions concerned the planets and the sun. These were important questions for me. My mother wanted to know something about health, and how we ought to nurture it. He replied with detailed medical knowledge. My questions about the sun and the planets were ones he replied to along with others' questions about the world of the stars.

My colleagues were more interested in mundane questions, while I took an interest in spiritual matters. I became a member of the Society and was then allowed to hear the members' lectures. Now I can understand that the other members thought I was too young. But Steiner said that it was fine for me to come along. Today I am so grateful that I was able to hear all this wisdom, which will remain forever in my soul.

We could not have been happier. No day went by without my teacher coming to show us new things. In the mornings we listened to talks by Rudolf Steiner, and in the evenings we listened to other lectures. De Jong and Unger gave good lectures. They spoke on interesting subjects, such as the stars and mathematics, as well as on plants and other themes in the lecture programme. We could also practise painting with plant colours, which I enjoyed.

A private conversation

Now I want to continue describing my time in Dornach. Strangely, my colleagues did not seem to need experiences of reincarnation—like those I had—to follow what Rudolf Steiner was saying. I was able to understand him better, though, because I could recall two of my former lives. These were my life with you as my younger brother, and my life as a Crusader. This helped me to understand him better.

I had a private conversation with him, during which he said that I should learn to paint. I did, and later I was able to make a living by painting portraits and nature.

I painted a picture based on a motif in the Mystery Plays. It was exhibited in Dornach, and went on tour to Berlin too. This was after Rudolf Steiner's death, when we travelled to Italy and Berlin to speak of the work we were doing. Those were good times.

My mother died in a car accident. I was there when a driver lost control of his car and ran her over. This was such a painful event. Another woman was standing next to her and was also killed. My mother had meant everything to me.

The Goetheanum fire

Now I stopped living in Arlesheim and moved to Dornach instead. There I lived with an anthroposophical family. They were also watchmen at the Goetheanum, and it was the head of the family who first noticed that the Goetheanum was burning one night. This was still more terrible than my mother's death had been.

It had never occurred to us that this could happen, that the whole Goetheanum would burn down one night. It was really terrible. We had to stand by and watch as all we had built went up in smoke. We were devastated, and everyone was weeping. Rudolf Steiner alone remained calm. The only thing left standing was the chimney. We just couldn't grasp what had happened. But our thoughts soon turned to rebuilding the Goetheanum. I now had the skills I had learned from Martin Unterberg, who was no longer alive.

Now a period began when all work was focused on clearing away the ruins left by the fire. This was terribly unpleasant. We cried the whole time. We started to feel guilty for not guarding the Goetheanum better. But the arsonists had been so ingenious, lighting the fire between the interior and exterior wall so that the fire could spread unhindered without anyone noticing. By the time we did, the whole building was in flames, and the fire had been burning for many hours.

We were so sad, but Rudolf Steiner immediately set about planning the new Goetheanum. For us this was the greatest possible consolation. It was to be made of concrete and thus impossible to burn down. Everyone wanted to help with this new building. During construction of the first Goetheanum I had learned so much that I could now be of more use. The concrete had to be shaped in wooden moulds, and I was able to instruct others in how to do this.

Rudolf Steiner held many lectures that I was able to attend, and I also joined the First Class of the School of Spiritual Science.

My time in Dornach was very eventful. My mother died, the Goetheanum burned down and I became an anthroposophist. It may be that no one experienced these events as intensely as I did. I do not know, since I had no one I could discuss them with.

Hilke asks whether I had any friend I could talk to. But I didn't. We worked together and attended lectures together, but we could scarcely have private conversations with one another. The others could not help being gravely affected by the Goetheanum fire, but they were at least able to discuss it with each other, whereas my poor German meant that I couldn't find the right words. I had always spoken Italian with my mother. Now, after Rudolf Steiner died, I wanted to return to Italy.

My time in Italy and Paris

My mother had money in a bank account in Italy. I wanted to collect this money, but it had disappeared. My relatives had taken it when they needed food during the war. I could understand this, but now I wanted to get it back. I did so, and was able to buy myself clothes and a flat in Paris. I lived there for several years, making a living by helping on various building projects. This was a lovely time with many good friends. Many of them could speak a little German or Italian.

My friends all knew some myths relating to yin and yang and other esoteric movements, but they were unfamiliar with anthroposophy. I had to tell them about it and they were very interested indeed. My accounts were translated into French and disseminated in written form. I have bright, beautiful memories of this period. I did not always choose my words so well, but my friends understood their deeper meaning. Then I made contact with various people who had heard Rudolf Steiner speak in Paris, and we became good friends.

My relatives in Italy came to visit me and wanted to take me back to Italy so as to renew the now rather distant connections and hear my accounts of anthroposophy.

I taught increasingly, and earned an income by this means. My colleagues also wanted to have painting lessons, and I was able to sell several paintings.

But now the Second World War was approaching and I no longer had any money for painting and nice lectures. My colleagues and I lost our jobs and I bought flowers and sold them to a few older people who needed encouragement. But my income was too small, and so I tried to paint portraits of bank directors who paid well. My Jewish friends put me in contact with them.

My time in Hamburg

Now I wanted to return to Switzerland, but they no longer let in foreigners. My good friends obtained a temporary passport for me until I could get back to Germany where most of my friends now lived, in Hamburg. There one could paint and exhibit one's pictures in various places. That was nice, but we didn't have enough to eat and had to spend all our time trying to earn money. We did this by going to all the downtrodden people and selling flowers that we grew ourselves. That way we earned a little money and could buy our daily bread. But this wasn't enough in the long term, and it was my friend Gustav who sorted out the food problem by selling our paintings to German banks in Munich and Berlin. It was our Jewish friends who made this possible.

This saved us, as we had nowhere to live and were just living in houses in Hamburg that stood empty because their Jewish owners had fled. And we were friends and could live there until the house was confiscated by the Nazis.

Many people tried to emigrate to America where they had friends and relatives. My closest friends wanted to stay in Germany and hide until Hitler had been vanquished. They could not believe that anyone really wished to kill them just because they were Jews. It seemed beyond belief. But we hid them and had no idea that we were putting ourselves in danger by doing so.

The final period and the concentration camp

I had been given a house by Jews who had left Germany. It had a good cellar where I was able to hide several Jews. My friend Gustav had a similar house with a good cellar where he was able to accommodate two Jewish couples. Together we wanted to study anthroposophy. They were all Class members and we read the Class Lessons together from beginning to end. A Jewish Class reader gave us a book containing the Class texts before he was caught by the Gestapo. He did not want the texts to fall into the hands of the Nazis.

We were able to read them every evening and meditate together on them. It was very fine! We were able to meditate better than ever before because we did not know how long we would be able to go on doing so. As far as our inner life was concerned, this was the most fruitful time of our lives.

The Jews I hid were a little different from me. They wanted to hear what I knew about Polish history. I had studied this subject for I wished to understand my dreams of Åland, which I could recall during my time in Hamburg. My friends wanted to understand why Hitler had been able to inveigle some of the Poles to collaborate in the Third Reich. I was unable to tell them. But now I understand these were just rumours. The Poles were forced to collaborate.

My friends also wanted to know whether I could prove that Christ was really resurrected, but I was unable to prove it. They were of course Jews, but anthroposophists, and they understood anthroposophy, but not that Christ had overcome death. They could understand reincarnation, but were able to do so without understanding Christ's resurrection.

Now I had reason to reflect on this. Christ had once walked upon the earth. But without his resurrection we could no longer have reached the spiritual world after death, for we would then have been too tied to the earth to lift ourselves into spiritual spheres. This was an insight that I now gained.

My neighbour had a great deal of money, which we all now lived from; and my friends were quite certain that they would survive this time in their hide-away if we didn't tell anyone that they were there.

But one day the Gestapo fetched me and interrogated me. Someone had made an accusation. I kept silent although they struck me, kicked me between the legs and taunted me. They said they would let me go if I told them where they could find more Jews. But I told them I didn't know where more were. Then they took me to Bergen-Belsen and I underwent such torture that I went out of my mind, and they were able to prise out of me where my friends were hiding. This was so awful that I didn't want to be born again. I died while they were torturing me.

Gustav and I betrayed our friends. This happened under torture, and neither of us wanted to be reborn so as to avoid ever doing something like that again. The Jews we betrayed are now incarnated again in various countries, and I don't know where.

When I arrived in the world of spirit I did not want to be reborn again. I did not wish to be in a situation where I might betray my very best friends. But Christ encouraged me to remain a part of human evolution.

You can't fully understand how painful it was to betray them while being tortured to death by the Gestapo. This was much worse than the pain I suffered during interrogation. You can have some sense of it because we were such intimate friends through meditating on the Class Lessons together. I'm sure they did not understand how I could have betrayed them. That's the worst of it. They probably only heard that I had accused them, without knowing it happened under torture. And the Jews were gassed, without being tortured beforehand. You hope that they will eventually understand, and that we can be friends again. I hope so too. You can ask Christ to help. If I had betrayed them immediately they wouldn't have tortured me to death. I would then have revealed where they were straight away and would have avoided all the torments. Then they would have been caught sooner. During the first interrogations I was still able to resist the interrogators, despite slaps and kicks. I was so stupid that I thought I could stay silent whatever they did to me. But when they tortured me I couldn't. I lost all capacity for judgement.

The most important thing was that Christ saw and could comfort me. This made it possible for me to recover after death and to live on now without being utterly crushed all my life. My friends entered the concentration camp and were gassed. If I hadn't hidden them, we could not have read the Class Lessons together.

My friends were gassed before I was tortured. I have now learned this. It is an incredible easing of my conscience.

Memories of the Crusades

We could not remember that we had already been together in an earlier life. My Jewish friends were my superiors in my life in Palestine during the Crusades. They helped me to become a Crusader. My best friend in Dornach, my dear Gustav, who was also tortured, was likewise one of them in Palestine. Now he too is incarnated, as a woman, but did not get autism because he wasn't so afraid of Ahriman. This was because Gustav's tormenters did not torture him for so long – he died almost immediately. He died when they smashed in his skull with a blacksmith's hammer, with repeated blows. Gustav was not a Jew but an Austrian. He had also been in Dornach, though only occasionally. We liked each other a great deal because he was such a good, modest person, and found it so easy to understand others. This made him everyone's friend. But he could understand that I didn't have any friends, and he tentatively sought to befriend me. One might say that it wasn't a friendship of equals, but we did complement each other well. A deep friendship formed between us.

Why I got autism

My book is nearly done now. But I still have to say that I was so frightened by Ahriman due to the cynicism of my torturers that I was unable to develop my nervous system for this life. Ahriman obstructed me. I was unable to see the constellation of Scorpion – which you have to in order to build up your nervous system. Now several of my senses function poorly. I see badly, I can't feel my own movements, I don't know when I've eaten enough, my sense of taste is limited, and I don't always know when I need the toilet.

But when you press my hand I can feel it, and control my movements. And then I can write on the computer as I am doing now. This is the best thing to have happened in my life. In this way I can speak to you now.

My thoughts are with all those who can't speak and might now be able to write with the help of honest, helping people who wish to learn to support us with FC. My books are not so remarkable. My good teachers just want me to say what I know as a result of having to live without being able to speak. My books will not be that well known because I can't put things as well as ordinary writers. But, on the other hand, I know things that most of you don't yet know. No one can check up on my memories of my former lives, but there will be many who recognize the time with Rudolf Steiner. These memories of mine will rekindle memories of this fruitful period. My brothers weren't there then, but they recall other lives when we were together.

Dornach again...

My mother kept wanting to visit the Goetheanum building site to see how it was getting on. We both wanted to have an overview. My mother thought it would become the most interesting building in the world. But my good mother never saw it finished. Now it can no longer be seen, but she would so much like to see something as magnificent again. She has to take a look at the new Goetheanum. She has to go and see the new Goetheanum. We must also drive there and look at it. It was never finished in my day.

At the time there were many of us who wanted to become anthroposophists, but Rudolf Steiner wished us to ponder carefully on whether we really wanted to join the Anthroposophical Society. No doubt he had some intimation of the difficulties we would encounter later in life. We all witnessed how Hitler prohibited anthroposophy and began to persecute us. Some of us—like Martin—ended up in concentration camps because they were found with anthroposophical texts. I landed there because I had hidden my friends, who were Jews. I no longer remember their names.

My mother was also interested in anthroposophy, and became a member soon after I did. She has not yet been born again, but is preparing a life in a different country.

Ahriman wants to conquer the earth, but despite this we should help Ahriman by loving him for everything we receive from him. We can love him in such a way that he cannot harm us with his hatred. It is Christ who can help us do this.

7 Threshold Experiences

by Hilke, Andreas and Erik Osaka

(Originally Hilke Osika removed this from the main body of the text because it seemed too personal to her.)

Andreas: The reason why you sometimes feel ill is because you are coming close to the threshold of the spiritual world. But when you feel this you must give in to it and not cling tight to your body.

Martin: Hilke cannot pass over the threshold because she does not wish to give way to this when she feels it is possible. She ought to submit to it, accompanied by a mantra that runs: 'You can if you will.' Then you can enter the spiritual world. That is a good mantra for entering the world of spirit. You can meditate on it when you feel you are close to the threshold and experiencing that slight nausea which sometimes comes over you. It is the same for everyone.

Hilke (*a few days later*): Andreas, I removed the passage about feeling unwell in connection with the threshold, and that I shouldn't cling fast to my body — I thought it was too personal; but Martin thinks it ought to be included since these comments are relevant to others as well.

Andreas: It ought to be there, even if it strikes you as a little boastful. It really is important for many other people today. My version of the mantra runs: 'I can because I will it.' It is a matter of gaining insight into the spiritual world. This is so important for safely solving problems that we now have with the earth, poverty, hunger and nuclear power; and with poisons and toxins, and all economic problems.

Hilke: But Andreas, if I should succeed in having super-sensible perception, and this gave me greater insight into what ought to be done, I am not someone who could possibly have any influence on politics or on those who hold the reins of economic power.

Andreas: It's not important for you to do everything yourself, for otherwise there would be no point in perceiving supersensibly. When you enter the spiritual world you can do the right thing and warn people in positions of responsibility about their errors. Of course you would never wish to intervene in the freedom of others, and there's no need for you to influence anyone unless he is asking you for advice.

My spiritual teachers only give me advice if I ask them for it. And they all wish to bear responsibility for the advice which they give. Today everyone is seeking good advice, and no one has any good advice to give; but those in the world of spirit can respond to all questions. In the night, when people are asleep, they can ask their questions; and then those who see the answers in the spiritual world can give their replies. You can be one of those. You never bear responsibility in this way today when you give advice. But seen from the spiritual world, and giving your advice from the spiritual world, you bear greater responsibility.

There are not enough people who use prayer to enter the world of spirit. There is a great dearth of such people, and therefore it is important for more people to make efforts to come there. You are well placed to do this, but you still need to continue meditating for a good while yet on the necessary mantras which you have been preoccupied with for some time now. If you do this you will become able to support Christ's work on earth.

Andreas will encounter all this when he becomes responsible for his book.

It has to be avowed, so that more people can take this step. There is such a great need in the spiritual world, and likewise here on earth, for people desirous of spending time trying to enter the world of spirit. So many people just want to talk about their own problems in the spiritual world, and not address the problems of the whole earth.

Things can't go on like this—with no one taking responsibility for the earth as a whole. It may be that still more catastrophes must come first, but it would be better if everyone would try to meditate as you do, and to say that they wish to serve God's will. A great many more such people are needed. This isn't just some private matter that is fun to pursue. It ought to be a duty for all those who wish to be anthroposophists. Every effort is now needed: everyone who can learn to meditate is important. Erik descried how one meditates.

Erik: It is important to sit down calmly and quietly and reflect on a verse by a wise person. Instead of rushing on to the next thing, one needs to focus and dwell upon this thought for as long as one can hold it clearly in one's mind. You need to feel the words in your heart too. It is good to meditate every day. Five minutes are enough to begin with.

Andreas: I want to write more about my elemental beings. They wish you to use your gifts in this way, as far as possible, to meditate on the same mantra for a long while. Hilke has not yet been able to come to the right mantra, which runs: 'Amen, I will and so I can.' That is the mantra you should use if you feel you are approaching the threshold. Otherwise you will never cross it. At that moment you should no longer continue with the mantra you are momentarily engaged with, but picture God's will shining upon you like a great sun. Then you can cross the threshold.

That ought to be in my book too. Others can also experience coming close to the threshold, and use this mantra when their proximity to the threshold calls forth a certain kind of nausea. This is due to not being in one's body in the usual way. The difference here is that one does not feel sick due to eating or drinking something, but due to the content of meditation. One can sometimes feel this after reflecting on a spiritual matter. Then you can think of this mantra, and use it, and think of God as the sun, letting the sun shine upon you. But don't continue with the meditation text you were engaged in.

My angel thinks that you are often close to the threshold but it usually ends with you savouring this nausea, which you now know means you are close to the threshold, and breaking off the process. Now you know what you should do, and you can do it.

8 Waiting at the Threshold

Interview with Jos Meereboer
by Wolfgang Weirauch

Jos Meereboer, born 1948 in Schoorl (Holland), trained as a graphic designer and curative educator. Since 1979 he has worked in Germany as special needs teacher and tutor in anthroposophic institutions. He lives in Hamburg.

Among us live people who are quite different from most of us, and with whom it is initially difficult to make contact. These are people with autism. What secret surrounds such people, whose core individuality is as intact as anyone else, but who have all kinds of difficulties in connecting with their own bodily nature and the physical world of the senses?

To better understand people with autism, I had a detailed conversation with curative educator Jos Meereboer about the autistic world and its spiritual context.

Wolfgang Weirauch: Kanner first characterized autistic disorder in 1943, and in 1944 Asperger elaborated the autistic spectrum. What distinguishes the various forms of autism?

J. Meereboer: There's only one important difference, really. Kanner described severe forms of autism, whereas Asperger reported on milder ones. Asperger coined the term 'autistic psychopathy'. Of course there are various categories of autism, but it would be true to say that every autistic person is unique. On the one hand there are autistic people who are physically healthy while on the other there is autism caused by brain damage. There are also autistic children whose later symptoms originate in a lack of human care and attention in infancy. This is sometimes also called hospitalism. In addition there are children who have been sexually abused and show resulting autistic symptoms. They withdraw from their body and regard it as something alien to them.

W.W.: It is only in the past 50 years or so that people have been discussing autism. Did autism always exist or is it a more modern phenomenon?

J. Meereboer: Rudolf Steiner does not refer to autism in his Curative Education Course (CW 317)[*]. There is only a single case where Steiner speaks of a person's fear of fully incarnating—which is a similar condition to later accounts of autism. I cannot really give you an answer, but my gut feeling is that karmically caused forms of autism have always existed, though they may well have increased a good deal in recent times. In former times so-called handicapped people were often regarded as subhuman, and shut away or suchlike. But autism is certainly a phenomenon of our modern era, and its incidence is increasing.

When the industrial age began, Down's syndrome arose as a sort of counterpart or contrast to modern humanity. I suspect that many people with autism have prefigured

[*] *Education for Special Needs*, Rudolf Steiner Press 1998.

what is now starting to happen in society — in other words a kind of general social autism starting from the 50s and 60s of the last century. If one thinks how many people spend a great part of each day confined in front of the TV, PC or other media, no longer perceiving their surroundings or nature, or really engaging with current events, this is really autistic behaviour that has now become a social norm.

W.W.: Do you think it possible that forms of autism are caused by certain vaccines?

J. Meereboer: It's possible, but I have no detailed knowledge of it. For some children, some vaccinations do represent maltreatment of the physical body.

W.W.: So we can broadly distinguish two groups — those born with autism and those that acquire it for various reasons during their lifetime?

J. Meereboer: Yes, but the second group is not called autistic.

We live in two worlds

W.W.: Why are autistic people such a mystery?

J. Meereboer: This is largely because it's so hard for us to reach them, or for them to reach us. While it seems we all live in *one* world, autistic people, one can sense, live in two. This makes our relationship with them somewhat mysterious.

W.W.: Is there more autism amongst boys than girls?

J. Meereboer: Yes, but it's generally true to say there are more special needs males. This is because of the greater difficulty of male compared to female incarnation, since it engages more deeply with the earth.

W.W.: The old-fashioned term for such people is 'mentally handicapped', though nowadays we would probably say they are in need of 'special care' since a person's core individuality, his 'I', is never actually sick. Do we know how many autistic people belong to this group?

J. Meereboer: There is really no such thing as mental disability. The American psychologist Oliver Sacks, for instance, has given an account of the American woman Temple Grandin, who is autistic but also became a professor. She was unable to speak until the age of three, and showed a range of behavioural oddities, and was therefore diagnosed as having brain damage when she was two. There are many such autistic people. When conventional science refers to 'mental disability' this is only a label, for instance for young children sent to therapists, children whose autonomy is impaired. One cannot really understand autistic people by means of ordinary rationality, which is why they are so rarely treated in the way they should be. In anthroposophic institutions, of course, people do not assume that autistic people are 'handicapped'. This is because we know that the human 'I' can never be sick, but only the corporeal members into which it incarnates. The striking thing about most autistic people however is that these bodily sheaths are healthy but that the 'I' withdraws from them.

Plonked down language

W.W.: Some autistic people can speak while others don't. Can you say something about language in autism?
J. Meereboer: Many autistic people who do not speak could in fact do so but do not! When they speak, they usually do so without any feeling, very impoverished in emotion. Their language is monotonous. In my experience their sentences or words seem as though plonked down in front of them.
W.W.: How do we know that those who don't speak actually would be able to?
J. Meereboer: Because they have suddenly spoken at rare moments, and then fell silent again. If you examine their speech organs you find there is nothing organically wrong with them. There are also moments when they speak when alone, as some parents have reported.

W.W.: Why does their language strike you as 'plonked down' — rather like an external object?

J. Meereboer: Their language is something very externalized. Autistic people quite often confuse I and you — which is due to the fact that they have no sense of self or do not find this in relation to others. They have no sense of I. 'I' and 'you' are more or less arbitrarily confused and interchanged. People with autism can also refer to themselves by their own names.

Reversal of external and inner worlds

W.W.: Can you give an example to illustrate how autistic people confuse I and you?

J. Meereboer: If, for instance, an autistic person wishes to eat an apple, he might say: 'The apple must let itself be bitten' — for he cannot do this himself. He may look on as his sister bites into an apple, then he takes this apple and is faced by the same phenomenon, and might chuck the apple away. He wants the activity to emanate from the apple rather than from himself. This is a reversal very common in autistic people. Young autistic children often also stand on their heads instead of their feet.

The anthroposophic physician Walter Holtzapfel described this in much detail in his book *Children with a Difference: The Background of Steiner Special Education* (Lanthorn Press, 1995). Autistic people have no relationship with inner and outer, and this is key to understanding them. In anthroposophic terms, the external earthly world that we have around us during our lifetime becomes our inner world between death and a new birth, whereas our inner world as incarnated human beings becomes our outer surroundings after death. This is the reversal we all undergo between incarnation and excarnation. And if this reversal does not proceed properly in the next incarnation, we experience the world as autistic people do. It is as though they stand before an open door (the 'door of birth') but are unable or unwilling to pass through it. Or, in other cases, they stand at the threshold but can neither enter nor return. Or they have passed through the door but do not close the door behind them. These are the ones in whom autism only becomes apparent after the age of two or three. Pre-birth life and earthly life in some way merge into each other.

What this means is that autistic people always reverse or confuse inner life and outer world during their lifetime. Thus, involuntarily, they often do not know whether they are a you or an I: whether they are experiencing something inner or outer, whether they themselves should bite the apple or whether the apple itself should do something; or whether they should stand on their feet or their head.

W.W.: To what extent does this manifest in all autistic people?

J. Meereboer: We can see this to different degrees in each individual: there's a whole spectrum ranging from severe to slight. In some, the symptoms are only subtle, though occasionally they can come to very characteristic expression. For instance, you might take away a toy from a cupboard in an autistic child's bedroom that he hasn't played with for three years, but he notices it immediately. This is because he lives so strongly in the outer world.

W.W.: Do autistic people have a real life of feeling?

J. Meereboer: Outwardly their feelings are very impoverished, but inwardly this is not necessarily so — they are just unable to reveal their feelings to us.

W.W.: If we consider the phase of sensory experience and development of consciousness in infancy, what occurs in the early years — such as smiling at others, at the mother? How is their early visual contact with people?

J. Meereboer: It is often the case that children develop quite normally in the first two years, but before they start to say 'I' autistic symptoms suddenly appear. In my view this is due to a failed reversal from the non-earthly, pre-birth outer world into the earthly, inner world: this does not happen in a healthy way at birth but we only notice it when the child says 'I' of himself. In a person who develops normally, the moment arrives around the third year when the child feels himself to be an I, and the outer world as external to himself. This does not happen before then since the child is one with the external world for at least the first two years. The outer world is then, as it were, his pre-birth inner world, which is why we cannot yet see this distinction in an autistic child. An autistic child does however remain in this situation for longer.

One's own child a stranger

But in the first two years one can detect symptoms, such as the child not smiling, that suggest he might have autistic traits. Another such symptom is that eye contact does not seem fully human if the child does not recognize or perceive the mother as his mother. After just a few months, ordinarily, the child can smile and look you in the eye properly—but this is not so in an autistic child. Mothers also sometimes describe their child as being like a stranger. Rudolf Steiner tells us that children after birth directly perceive what their parents think. This is also true of autistic children, but they retain this capacity while it fades in other children.

W.W.: So they have a certain clairsentient or clairvoyant perception, and this is retained in later years?

J. Meereboer: Yes, as I said this is to do with the fact that they haven't relinquished their pre-birth life sufficiently. In pictorial terms, they remain at the threshold or sometimes take a small step forward. Really they stop at the door or do not shut it behind them. Healthy children shut the door some time between the ages of three and nine.

W.W.: Are there ways of finding out whether children retain clairvoyant gifts in later years?

J. Meereboer: This can only be done through Facilitated Communication using a computer. In outward communication with parents and others this can scarcely be discovered. But we ourselves should increasingly develop our consciousness soul* and also learn to perceive supersensibly, so that we can locate the spiritual conditions inhabited by the consciousness of autistic people. At present we are still wholly reliant on FC.

I recall a 16-year-old autistic boy, from a Camphill† home, who used FC to request that the class teacher he had from Class One be thanked, and to tell her that, although he never spoke a word, he had absorbed everything she taught. He sat there in utter silence through all the years, taking no apparent part in lessons. But he had a brilliant memory.

W.W.: A young child gradually finds his way into our world, and wants to perceive as much about it as possible: first he masters the world physically, then in later years engages with it in soul and spirit. How is this for an autistic person? Does he not fully engage with this world because of a failure to accomplish the reversal you mentioned?

J. Meereboer: The more the child connects with his body, and the better he does so, the more differentiated will be his perception of his surroundings. Incarnation is a process of synthesis while differentiated perception is one of analysis, following which we combine the details of things again in our ideas and thinking. This process does not occur in autistic people because they do not connect properly with their body. How, then, can they absorb perceptions of the outer world through their body? It is as if they were hanging outside their body. Apart from this,

---

* A developing faculty of the human soul.
† Homes for people with special needs, based on the medical insights of Rudolf Steiner.

they live far more in their outer environment than others, and since they already live 'out there' they do not feel any need to grow into their surroundings.

Living in their surroundings

W.W.: Can you describe this reversal in a little more detail?

J. Meereboer: In the fifth lecture of his Curative Education Course, Steiner speaks of the human organism, offering two different models of the human being. Model A has its I organization outside itself, then, as we progress inwards, the astral body, then the etheric body and finally the physical body. Then Steiner presents Model B, which is precisely the reverse: the I within us, the physical in the outer world (see illustration). In the head of an incarnated person we have Model B: the I inside. In the metabolic-limb organization we have Model A, with the I organization

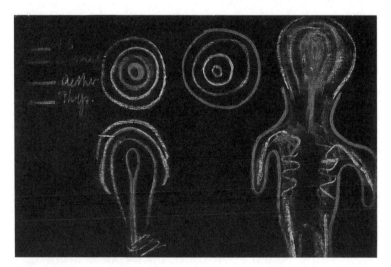

© *Rudolf Steiner Estate, Dornach 2011*

Rudolf Steiner, board drawings for the Curative Education Course, CW 317. Lecture 5, 30 June 1924

outside us. In other words, the I is centrally organized in the head, and peripherally organized in the limbs. With our head we look out into the external world and reflect it within our brain. With our limbs, our will life, by contrast, we grasp our will and realize a will impulse, an action, in the external world, giving rise to a real consequence in our environment.

By contrast, the autistic person turns away from his physical body as will organization. His physical body does not interest him, he remains in the outer world, doing nothing with his physical body. He dwells in what is around him—for instance the vacuum cleaner or the electric fan. I recall an autistic boy in Holland whose I, instead of sitting in his physical body, inhabited the planets. He could reel off all the planetary constellations and positions each day. An autistic person does not wish to use his physical body as an instrument but instead lives somewhere in his outer surroundings. This relates to the metabolic-limb system model.

It is somewhat harder to understand in the case of the head. Autistic people do not perceive the world around them in order to reflect it within. Instead they often connect with material things—which can also be intrinsic to the brain. But they do not use the brain as a reflective organ for perception and thinking processes, instead uniting primarily with things in the outer world. This gives rise also to symmetry compulsions, when they arrange everything in a careful row or, if one drawer is opened, have to open all the other drawers as well; or line up all the shoes of fellow residents in rows of left and right shoes. The most important thing for them is that clear order prevails in their surroundings—which ought not to be too extensive or open-ended. If one disrupts this order it hurts them and destabilizes them completely. You have to imagine this as if I were to enter your conceptual world and bring it into complete dis-

array. Autistic people have their conceptual world outside them, around them—for instance in their room—
rather than inside them.

They cannot will

And on the other hand they do not want to connect with
their body: in this sense they are not properly incarnated.
They do not use their body as an instrument and therefore
remain outside it in their surroundings. It is not true to say
that they 'cannot' or 'will not' but that they cannot will. If
they were able to accomplish this reversal, they would
immediately be able to use their body in a great many more
ways—to write, ride a bicycle, etc. But since they don't use
their body as an instrument, they do nothing with their
body. Often their organism is entirely healthy.

When I started working as a curative educator in Holland, I was surrounded by young men with autism; and
when they lay in bed and slept, they looked like young
princes, harmonious of countenance and finely formed.
This healthy aspect often came through when they swam
as well. But the moment they sit there in their room, they
start making compulsive and stereotypical movements,
trying to engage with their physical body in a cramped,
convulsive way. They are looking for some kind of secure
hold, and if they don't have it they are lost in their surroundings. Often they will shut themselves up in a small
room if it all gets too much for them.

So ultimately we can say that the inversion from the
spiritual into the physical world has not taken place in
autistic people. Non-earthly and earthly worlds are not
properly separated for them but transposed into each
other. This fills them with anxiety, makes them insecure,
for they cannot properly orientate themselves.
W.W.: It would be interesting to know what happens to
them after death, when this inversion occurs again. This

ought to be a world that is relatively normal for them since in a certain respect they were already familiar with it — albeit in a confused, combined form — while incarnated on earth.

J. Meereboer: Yes, it would be interesting to research this.

The attempt to experience oneself

W.W.: How does an autistic person use his senses?

J. Meereboer: An autistic person's senses are not disturbed during incarnation but they are externally governed, used differently. When we use our eyes to see we have to forget that we have eyes, and likewise forget we have ears when we hear. An autistic person relates to his eye as a thing that belongs to the body. 'Aha,' he says, 'what is this?' And then he presses his thumb on his eye to experience what it actually is.

W.W.: Why do autistic people often clap their hands, clap their hand to their ear or make other such movements?

J. Meereboer: Not all autistic people do this, but when they do I believe it is an attempt to engage with their physical body, to experience it. They are really asking whether the physical body belongs to them or not. It is a stereotype will impetus but not free will, an 'emergency' attempt to gain some sense of themselves.

W.W.: Is this compulsive or is it an attempt to perceive themselves through their physical body?

J. Meereboer: Really it is both. In a compulsive way they try to come into touch with the physical body. Here of course it would be interesting to know about the karmic embroilments affecting autistic people — whether, in their previous life for instance, they were victims in some way or perhaps also perpetrators, and suffered a great deal in consequence in kamaloka.

Disorder makes them anxious

W.W.: How does an autistic person harm himself?

J. Meereboer: He may bang his head against a wall. Often he may not even feel any pain, or at least one gets the sense that he doesn't. This would also mean that the astral body of autistic people is not properly in their physical body. But if you mess up their room this will really hurt them — a real soul pain! They need outward order. Disorder makes them anxious. Outer order is their only security on earth.

W.W.: Can we put it like this: that the order we create in our thinking, perhaps a certain view of the world, logical thinking, maybe even a belief system, is the same for us as order in the immediate external environment of an autistic person?

J. Meereboer: Yes, we can see it like that. In their wardrobe, for instance, clothes have to hang as they think they should. Everything has to have its fixed place. This gives them security, without which they flow out too much into their surroundings.

W.W.: What actually happens when one messes up an autistic person's room?

J. Meereboer: He will probably start raging, associated with great anxiety. One would not wish to inflict this on him.

W.W.: I don't wish to draw simplistic comparisons, but for a normal person with a very restricted and rigid world view, it would surely be good to muddle this up a little so as to bring him into movement and encourage him to think fresh thoughts. Would it be possible — very cautiously — to do this with autistic people too? Might it be helpful to bring a certain limited movement into his external sur-roundings?

J. Meereboer: I don't think there is any clear therapeutic programme for this, but you can gently make movements with the autistic person; and if at the same time one has supersensible capacities and knows what is going on in him, one might undertake such a thing. Each autistic person is individually different, however, and that should always be remembered.

It is similar with time schedules. If lunch is always at noon, autistic people cannot cope with it suddenly being at 1 o'clock instead. Unlike full earthly citizens, they have neither a proper spatial awareness nor a temporal one. It almost seems as if they live in the moment.

W.W.: Do they therefore have no sense of the future or the past?

J. Meereboer: No—many children I cared for did not.

W.W.: But if an autistic person has supersensible perception, surely he has an idea of the past and future, and maybe even of a previous life?

J. Meereboer: Certainly, but this would be a supersensible overview, which autistic people do indeed have. Perhaps one can picture it like this: that one learns a whole story and is then able to walk about in it. In this overall picture autistic people do know what happens before and what happens after.

W.W.: But you mean they have less of an inner feeling that, say, three years have passed?

J. Meereboer: This is hard for them, and you can see this when you say something like, 'I'm going to church tomorrow.' This doesn't mean anything to them. But this is only true of people with severe autism. I do know a boy with mild autism, though, who has no relationship to time, and will arrive at school when the school day is finished.

Future perceptions

W.W.: Is it not possible to tell autistic people that they are going to do this or that tomorrow, so that they look forward to it?

J. Meereboer: It's extremely difficult. At least, it is with most of them. But there are remarkable things such as the following: the parents of an autistic child phone the teacher up to say they will visit tomorrow, but the teacher does not tell the child. Nevertheless, he knows this. In Holland I had the following experience: an autistic child painted a picture showing that his former teacher would die in three days. And this is exactly what happened. He knew it beforehand. There is supersensible perception therefore of what is coming in the future. By contrast they do not experience the external flow of time, and have no relationship with time sequences. This really is a strange world. The first time you engage with such things they have a dramatic quality: you come into contact with a world that really only causes you pain.

The most important therapy for an autistic person is to be accepted as autistic. If one doesn't accept this, he does not feel secure, and grows anxious.

W.W.: And does anthroposophic curative education see it like this?

J. Meereboer: An average anthroposophical curative educator knows that there is no such thing as 'mental disability', that the core individuality, the I, is always healthy. At most, ignorance might lead to excessive efforts to 'cure' an autistic person so that he 'functions' properly, and that some impatience arises during these efforts. A curative teacher's task is, certainly, to try to guide children in need of special care in the right direction and address their problems. But you can't do this for autistic people: you have to do it *with* them. You can't simply compel them. There are various therapies, e.g. massage, to help them feel their body, and compresses for young children—but one always has to sense whether each autistic person accepts this treatment, or whether it is too much for him. The professor described by Oliver Sacks did this voluntarily: she developed a pressure machine which she went into to be able to feel her own body.

Percept and concept

W.W.: I have also read that autistic people observe various objects in their surroundings very precisely — such as a chair from all sides, also from underneath. Are they using their whole body to do something that others do only with their senses, for instance the sense of sight or touch?

J. Meereboer: Those are autistic people who have stayed further back in the world of spirit, who really haven't arrived on earth at all. They have no relationship to the objects we have around us, no concept of them. They do not see that something is a chair we can sit on; and if they wish to know what sort of object it is, they have to look at it from all angles, from below too. Nor do they see, for instance, that a fan in the window is something that supplies fresh air, perceiving instead only its rotating movement.

W.W.: For a properly incarnated person the world is divided in his awareness into two realms — the various perceptions of the sensory world that stream towards him chaotically, and which have no intrinsic connection with each other, and on the other hand the concepts of his thinking which create connections. What we call knowledge arises as a combination of these two aspects. In *The Man Who Mistook His Wife for a Hat,* Oliver Sacks also describes an academic who was unable to accomplish this process of cognition — in other words to connect separate sensory impressions with corresponding concepts. It seems to me that autistic people tend to do something similar.

J. Meereboer: Yes. I can give a clear example of this: an autistic person is sitting at a table. A bell rings but he does not react. One might think that he is deaf but in fact he hears the bell perfectly well. He just cannot connect the concept 'bell' with the tone he hears. And if he doesn't know what is ringing, why should he react? There are many noises after all. And since there are too many noises, it all gets too much for him. Chaos arises in autistic people from the many perceptions for which they cannot form concepts, which they cannot organize and integrate through their thinking. One must try to ensure therefore that they are not exposed to too many impressions.

W.W.: If autistic people tend not to be able to connect external perceptions with concepts, how can one help them to better connect these two realms in an act of cognition?

J. Meereboer: By experiencing things together with them. In the example of the bell one has to make the bell visible and ring it, and then they ought to be able to connect it with the ringing sound. But this always depends on the severity of autism in each person. There is a whole spectrum between very mild and very severe. It is certainly good — for all of us of course — to develop interest in the external, earthly world, since this becomes our inner world after death. And efforts in this direction are therefore a precondition for healthy incarnation in one's next life. One could gradually but repeatedly encourage an autistic person to take an interest in his surroundings, though always without compulsion. For instance, it is helpful for adults with autism to have purposeful work or activity of some kind. In Holland I knew an autistic child with a very one-sided talent, already in infancy, for building towers of wooden blocks with extraordinary precision, so that they didn't fall down. When he grew up he was able to use this gift of precision in making lyres, because he worked so carefully. This was a purposeful activity he could engage in, and this sense of professionalism helped him become a real citizen of the earth.

Perceiving from the periphery

W.W.: How do autistic people perceive other people?

J. Meereboer: Like a young child, or perhaps like an

angel—at any rate not through their body. Looking at you now I'm using my body; but when I fall asleep and my soul and spirit leave my body, I do not use it when I look at you. That's roughly how you can picture it in the case of an autistic person. This is also why he can learn a great deal at school.

W.W.: But this would mean that his soul is very connected with others. We always hear that autistic people have no contact with others. Is this only apparently the case?

J. Meereboer: In a broader sense they certainly dwell in the soul of the other person, but a real encounter between two people, from I to I, can only occur through the body, and this is something autistic people can't do.

W.W.: Would someone with autism perceive severe psychological suffering in another person in the same room?

J. Meereboer: Definitely. Autistic people have feelings but cannot express them. Birger Sellin, a man with autism, also said this. In his book, entitled *I Don't Want to be Inside ME Anymore*[*] he writes:

> It was Christmas again—a festival full of harmony—the crazy festivity in uniquely elaborate illusion-ritualized patterns—i turn my loving thanks to you i was so very glad.

And in relation to the reversal phenomenon we described above, he makes the following interesting statement:

> one thing is crazy—being in oneself is a dead condition—without oneself is loneliness—can live neither in-oneself nor without-oneself—there are no pure states—always a change takes place in me—even to work in peace—two powers that don't unite.

This is the situation of reversal, which he also experienced.

---

[*] Birger Sellin: *Ich will kein inmich mehr sein*, Cologne 2005.

When we incarnate we perceive the other through our senses. An autistic person scarcely perceives the other through his senses but instead from the periphery. He perceives you as Wolfgang Weirauch from the periphery and knows exactly what you are thinking and feeling, everything. But he is scarcely able to process this individually in himself, and has no personal relationship to what he perceives. He simply perceives something objective.

W.W.: But how objective is such supersensible perception?

J. Meereboer: That is precisely the question. It may involve a certain registering of what he perceives without him necessarily being able to make much of it outwardly.

W.W.: To what extent is the will disturbed in autism? Are autistic people unable to speak, or don't they want to?

J. Meereboer: This is all connected with them turning away or withdrawing from their corporeality.

W.W.: What does this actually mean?

J. Meereboer: They are unable to attend to their body, which is likely to be because they don't wish to incarnate. For that reason they don't identify with their body — and without corporeality one cannot activate the will. In therapy one can of course try to connect autistic people with their bodies, but such attempts — using massage, warmth therapies and similar — are just a tentative approach to the problem.

W.W.: Warmth is also an interesting factor in relation to autistic people. Is it true that autistic children seem more 'normal' when they have high temperatures?

J. Meereboer: Yes, that is indeed true.

W.W.: Can you say something about the fact that many autistic people appear to be very intelligent, can read complex words at a young age, and later reel off whole pages of a book by heart?

J. Meereboer: In general we can say that children cope in diverse ways with their disability. The intelligence of autistic people has nothing to do with their body but with what they bring with them karmically. Birger Sellin, for instance, projected his being into his father's bookshelf, absorbing the books through capacities different from normal ones, and teaching himself to read.

W.W.: But if he learned to read like this and absorbed the content of the books, he must have engaged with the physical world since a book is printed and exists physically!

J. Meereboer: That's right. And, to be honest, I don't understand it either. I only know that instead of taking hold of their bodies and using them as you or I do, their being is out in their surroundings. In some way or other the contents of a book imprint themselves in an autistic peson's etheric body. This is likely to involve photographic memory too. We have to read each word, one after the other, to get a sense of the whole, whereas many autistic people can do this at a glance. This too is a reversal phenomenon: to look upon the content of a book from outside and then absorb it. This is something similar to the life panorama that arises as the etheric body dissolves after death. An autistic person can summon this overview of contents.

W.W.: To what extent do autistic people experience love and sexuality?

J. Meereboer: In severe forms of autism, as I experienced this in Holland, these are more or less non-existent. They do manifest in milder forms of autism, but always with little feeling or emotionality. I recall a boy who was in a love with a girl — but he related to her rather like an object.

W.W.: But was he really in love with her?

J. Meereboer: That's what he said. He showed interest in the girl because she struck him as pretty. But after one or two months this supposed feeling of love had faded again. He only confided in me, though, and did not tell the girl. I had the sense that it was something that belonged to his age and that he needed to project it on some girl or other. It was very much in his head.

W.W.: And what about sexual needs?

J. Meereboer: This isn't something I have seen. A sexual need, after all, can really only arise if one has a relationship with one's own body.

W.W.: But they do live in a body, still. They must feel hunger — or not even that?

J. Meereboer: There are autistic people who eat too little and others who eat too much. As carer and keyworker one has to work with this in a focused way, sometimes rather as one does with young children.

She sat under the table and pretended to be a tiger

There's another thing I have observed: it is very helpful for an autistic person to have a Down's syndrome child in his close vicinity. Someone with Down's syndrome does not ask for much but actually gives out love, and in my view such children are precisely the reverse of autistic children. I once gave a lecture on autism in Slovenia, and someone asked what one could do with autistic people who never come to a meal. I suggested that one could establish a connection between children with Down's and autistic children by getting them to eat together, and that the latter would then come to meals.

A lady in the audience immediately confirmed this. She said that an autistic boy had never appeared for meals but that now, since a boy with Down's syndrome was present, he always came on time. This is due to the fact that a child with Down's invites autistic children in a certain way without demanding. Such a person does not interfere in an autistic child's will by wanting something of the autistic person in a way that tries to compel him.

For instance, I know an autistic girl who did not want to participate in school lessons, who didn't come to school because the new environment was far too threatening for her. She just sat under a table and pretended to be a tiger, keeping everyone at bay. I suggested to her that she could help a Down's syndrome girl in the same class. She immediately agreed, went to lessons and learned everything she could. This would not have happened without the Down's syndrome child. I therefore consider it a very important and effective therapeutic approach to bring people with Down's syndrome and autism together.

Failed incarnation

W.W.: The whole phenomenon of autism appears as failed incarnation. What causes some people to choose an incarnation in which they have next to no connection with other people and their surroundings?

J. Meereboer: It is probably the case in much autism — as other curative educators confirm — that people come to the earth with this disorder because they suffered traumatic experiences in their last life.

Fear of entering the world

Frau Staël von Holstein channelled a conversation I was able to have with Etshevit (a tree spirit; see *Nature Spirits of the Trees*, Floris Books 2009). He confirmed this, and also said that many autistic people were sexually abused in their last life. This might of course also involve other forms of physical abuse such as torture etc. And this can fill those who become autistic with fear of entering the world again in case they have to experience such things once more. Reticence or wariness of modern civilization and the current state of humanity — in other words crass materialism and widespread coldness in social relationships — may also play a major part in mild forms of autism. When a soul of this kind is preparing for incarnation, it is understandable that he is wary of incarnating in such conditions and might prefer to remain in the world of spirit.

W.W.: In asking the following question I feel I am skating on thin ice since I have no overview of what's involved – but maybe you can find an answer. If we assume that someone was sexually abused or tortured in a previous life, and then has an autistic incarnation, how does the cause-effect aspect of karma work here? Is it the case that sexual abuse or torture works as cause to bring about an inevitable effect of autism in the following incarnation? This would be very unjust. Or is it the case that in a subsequent life a person will voluntarily seek this autistic incarnation due to experiences in the previous life?

J. Meereboer: In many people a new incarnation involves redress and rebalancing, associated with each person's individual destiny. But in my view, autistic incarnations are caused by fear of incarnating: such a soul does not want to have to experience again what it already experienced. But they have to come to earth, and this gives rise to a great need to find a connection with Christ. And this is then also a compensation for the next life. This is why it is important to help autistic people to find a connection with Christ in curative homes, for instance through acts of worship. One has to keep guiding them back to Christ.

In a certain sense autistic people are also in contact with Ahriman, perhaps more strongly than other people. We can see this in their intense interest in technical matters, and also in the fact that everything in their lives is automatic and schematic and that they have little inclination towards life itself and etheric processes. We should therefore repeatedly bring them into touch with Christ; and actually they have a stronger longing for Christ because of their increased contact with Ahriman.

From my own experience I can say that no autistic child attending the Children's Service* has ever yet responded verbally to the petition 'The spirit of God will be with you if

---

* A special service of the Christian Community church.

you seek him'. Normally children say, 'I will seek him.' A girl I am thinking of was never able to say this. When I asked her about this, she said, 'I don't want to seek him, but I want him to be with me always.' She was unable to will or seek, and this situation made her anxious. So she did not respond to the petition but did know, nevertheless, that Christ is always with her and that someone who is with you does not need to be sought. She had already found him.

Little interest in life

W.W.: Can you say something about an autistic person's etheric body? Is it connected too firmly or too loosely with the physical body? Or to what extent does autistic inflexibility inform the way his etheric body is configured?
J. Meereboer: When we incarnate, the I gradually configures an individual, physical body based on the model inherited from our parents. The etheric body is used to build the body and sustain its life, while the astral body serves, for instance, to form ideas. In severe autism the I scarcely has any way of engaging with these three bodies. The etheric body has a little autonomous impetus. Someone with severe autism has no interest in his etheric body (life body) and therefore none either for what is alive around him — e.g. plants and animals.

I can't make much of the idea of an inflexible etheric body. At most, one could say that the etheric body is not individualized. Something similar can be seen clearly in the physical body: autistic people often have no individual expression in their physical body, especially none in their faces when they are asleep. When they are awake, in contrast, the face is often distorted.

The astral body is not really governed, which is why sufferers of autism cannot sufficiently protect themselves through their life of soul against things they are exposed to.

For example they are easily alarmed because they cannot integrate certain perceptions. Above all, though, the I has only a small capacity to work upon the three lower members, and so these accomplish too little of what they ought to.

W.W.: Can you say a little more about anxiety in autism?

J. Meereboer: The most important thing to convey to autistic children is that we are trustworthy and reliable. Nothing will work, really, without this basis of trust. It can take a year or so, however, to establish it. And the most important precondition for it is our acknowledgement and acceptance of their autism. We also have to make clear to them that we won't hold it against them when they get in a rage—since they can't help it. I once looked after a boy who got a tick bite and was so alarmed that something could happen to him as a result that he started dismantling the whole classroom. There is absolutely no point in being angry with him in this situation or punishing him. The only thing that helps is taking him to the doctor as fast as possible, and then he can calm down again.

W.W.: Is anxiety and fear very common in autistic people—even on a daily basis?

J. Meereboer: As basic predisposition it is really always present. In Holland I once witnessed a very strange form of fear in an autistic child: the whole day through he saw odd beings sitting on the sofa. This wasn't a problem during the day, but they frightened him in the evening before he fell asleep. Then one had to open the window and ask the beings to leave. After this the young man was able to fall asleep.

He stood before the threshold

When I was young I had a very interesting experience in Holland with another autistic boy. I was coming back with him from a shopping trip, taking a path that ran beside the dunes, when we saw a twig lying in front of us on the path. The boy stopped in front of it — it was like a barrier for him. I picked the twig up and threw it into the bushes. But he went to find it in the bushes and put it back on the road, remaining stuck on the other side of it. What does one do if this happens?

W.W.: I have no idea.

J. Meereboer: The world was divided for him into two realms, as at birth. He stood before the threshold and his consciousness would not let him pass. It was no good removing the threshold. Instead I went back to the village with him, then returned on the other side of the street. This time we could pass the twig. He knew this boundary was still there but he was able to go past it on the other side of the path. Strange things like that are common experiences with autistic people.

W.W.: People with autism often don't look you in the eye but, when they do, are they telling you they want to hear more from you?

J. Meereboer: It varies. I know many who look at you with a fixed gaze and won't look away until you have answered them.

W.W.: So they want to use this eye contact to ensure you recognize what they want without them saying it?

J. Meereboer: Yes. However, this is not a warm gaze illumined by the I, but a fixed stare.

W.W.: We have already talked about stereotype modes of behaviour in autistic people, when they carry out actions in a rigid and ordering way — for instance lining up objects in a row etc. As far as I have understood, they often carry out such actions very fast. Is this because they think they don't have any time, or are they just very skilled at such things?

J. Meereboer: In my view they don't live in temporal processes but in time units, in bars. When we do something as non-autistic people, we usually start with an initiating phase followed by a longer main phase and a concluding end phase. Or we allow ourselves a little time, get an overview of a situation and let things develop. People with autism really have no relationship to such temporal processes and usually therefore whatever they do has to be done immediately. I also know many autistic children who draw something very quickly — and then it's finished, done with. There is no developmental process involved, and that is why it all happens so fast.

W.W.: As a parent, can one do anything to ameliorate autism if one notices signs of it in the first three years?

J. Meereboer: The chief thing is to avoid using force on an autistic child. One can do all one can to try to help the child develop a stronger relationship with his physical body. This can be done by stroking, playful interaction, and by grasping hold of things together. But one must always take care that such children also want this or are able to want it — for if not they will shout or cry out. One notices this immediately. Things can easily become too much for them. Such exercises and processes are healthy for all children of course, to help them form a stronger relationship to their body. In later years this can be achieved through massage.

W.W.: How is it with embraces and similar demonstrations of love. Do autistic children want this?

J. Meereboer: Embraces are often too much for them and too close, but of course they need a great deal of love. This can be very problematic for mothers, though, because they get no responses to their loving gestures.

Creating a relationship with time

W.W.: Is it a good idea to remove autistic children from their home, and place them in a community of other autistic children?

J. Meereboer: If the autistic child is an only child, and his parents are the only ones close to him, this may just reinforce the isolation he already experiences. It only works in a residential community if the autistic children trust those who care for them; and this in turn is only true if those with autism feel their carers understand and accept them as they are. Naturally one should be careful not to remove autistic children too early from their family relationships—there is no hard and fast rule for this. However, the advantage of a community is that such children can gain a better relationship to time through the rhythmic sequence and schedules of the day, week and month, especially through seasonal festivals. A religious orientation in the recurring seasonal festivals is particularly important. It is still better if this community includes children with Down's syndrome. And if one offers religious services, such as Christian Community or nondenominational ones, and they can develop trust in these rites, they feel very secure in them. The overarching being of such a community, its angel, also gives help, trying to ensure that all its members interact in a way that makes all secure.

The child study is an outward aid as well. Here all the carers of a particular child focus their attention on him and try to understand him properly. This has a strong therapeutic effect. Of course it has to be done properly.

However, I can also understand the autistic people who no longer wish to be part of any community—and this is always so when they don't feel properly understood.

W.W.: Is it right to treat autistic children as if they were older than they are?

J. Meereboer: The way one relates to children and the content of things said should always be age-appropriate. Psychologically though, one has to meet them where they are. This is very problematic with autistic children since it is hard to know where they stand. In some way they stand nowhere. We can really only meet them where they are in their compulsive or automatic actions. But I would always relate to them in age-appropriate ways. When they are five or six, they need fairy tales just like others of that age. One can certainly base teaching on the Waldorf curriculum.

Their mother is often only a thing for them

W.W.: You stressed that many autistic children often devote their interest to the inorganic world. But don't they also perhaps have a relationship with spiritual, artistic and religious concerns? Is it perhaps true that they cannot express their interest in these realms and that one should guide them towards an experience of them?

J. Meereboer: Perhaps the term 'interest' is the wrong one; they either have a relationship to something, or none. They usually have no relationship to the living world. This is not true, though, in milder autism. Naturally it would be a fine thing if one were able to convey the sense of such a relationship to them.

W.W.: So it would be wrong to give them a rabbit to care for?

J. Meereboer: Very probably, for they might well torment the rabbit without noticing they were doing so. If they have a plant in their room they might pick at it and chuck it away. Relationships with people are similarly difficult; they may not notice that they are hurting someone else. Their mother is often only a thing for them. They need her only to fulfil functions but not because they love her unreservedly. If they want a glass of water to drink, for instance, they need their mother like a tool because they can't put the glass to their lips on their own. They take their mother's hand, lead it to the glass, and then the mother lifts the glass to the child's mouth. It is similar to Facilitated Communication: they need the mother's will.

W.W.: Can you say something about autistic people's artistic gifts?

J. Meereboer: They usually have no artistic gift, with one exception: they are musical. They express this however in unrhythmic ways. Usually they can't get anywhere much with the pictorial arts. When they paint, the outcome is always very static. But it is good if we introduce them to religious artworks. In general it is important for them not only to hear about religion but for this to be mediated through music and artistic activity.

W.W.: Wouldn't it be good for them to do clay modelling?

J. Meereboer: Yes, certainly. If they can do this it gives them a stronger connection to their body. I knew an autistic boy who was good at turning vases in a pottery. But he produced identical vases for years, without any creative imagination. The person I referred to earlier, who made lyres with great precision, could never have designed a lyre himself.

W.W.: What is the memory of autistic people like? Is it true to say that they have many memories present in their awareness simultaneously, as in life after death?

J. Meereboer: Yes, it's similar. Superficially people always think that they have an extraordinary memory. They glance at a book and might be able to describe or present its whole content—if they did such things. They know its contents. I am also sure that a great many autistic people are clairvoyant and can read thoughts if such thoughts are formulated precisely enough. They are similar in this way to children in the first two years of life.

W.W.: Is it also true that they cannot properly structure their brains when they are young?

J. Meereboer: Yes. If their movement apparatus is disturbed so that they do not properly move—when 'I' and astral body for instance cannot take a proper hold of the physical body—then the brain cannot be properly structured or formed. This is something we see in other special needs children, sometimes even in more severe form. It must be similar in autistic children because they often do not properly or fully move. It would be good for autistic children to move in as differentiated a way as possible, but they do not let this happen!

Rescuing them from an uninhabited island

W.W.: Autistic people can learn to converse with others via FC, computer-aided communication. What exactly does the helper do here?

J. Meereboer: I myself have no experience with it but basically the helper aims to provide support so that the autistic person can engage his will—which he can't do on his own. This is done by supporting his arm so that he can press on the keys. One gives him one's own will so that he can begin to operate the keyboard. In a higher or super-sensible sense he can already do this, but he cannot use his body to do so. This is why one has to help him to use his body for this activity, for this skill, and then he can make use of the dead tool of the computer. As helper, though, you have to keep your own will completely out of it, for otherwise what the autistic person communicates may be tinged. Thus one holds his arm and the autistic person seeks the letters himself.

W.W.: Let's assume that there are more autistic people now than there used to be, even if we can never be sure of this. They live imprisoned due to traumas from a previous life and other reasons; and now it becomes possible for them to express themselves through the computer. Autistic people are more or less clairvoyant, live in their prison and cannot express themselves—cannot tell people what they want to say. Suddenly they are able to express themselves through the computer, breaking out of their imprisonment, and conveying by this means what they actually think and perceive. If such a thing becomes possible for them all of a sudden, what will this be like for them?

J. Meereboer: It's like a miracle, and certainly a blessing that this enables them to gain access to other people. It liberates them from their prison, their isolation. It must of course be an absolute relief for them, a liberation, like being reborn. It is like being rescued from an uninhabited island. Suddenly they can communicate with those around them.

W.W.: Do you believe that a great many autistic people have clairvoyant gifts?

J. Meereboer: I cannot really tell but I suspect this is so. However, these are not clairvoyant capacities acquired on earth since in general autistic people acquire no skills on earth, or only very few. If they have clairvoyant capacities they are really telling us about things they know from their previous life or from the life between death and a new birth. What they acquire in this life is minimal, although they do of course gain a sense of things around them in this life in a kind of supersensible state. The thing that helps them enormously is to lead them towards Christ, and give them confidence that they will be able to live normally again in a subsequent life.

W.W.: To what extent do they have a clairvoyant overview of all modern phenomena and the world we now inhabit? Do they only supersensibly read what people around them are thinking, or would they be able for instance to know something clairvoyantly about Peru although no one they know is thinking about it?

J. Meereboer: Maybe they could, but probably they don't do this. They are often only preoccupied with what is around them or what occurred in their previous life. And I presume that primarily they only perceive the thoughts of people they have something to do with. But if autistic people knew us both, I am sure they could also perceive what we are talking about together here, and what we are thinking about now.

Clairvoyance

W.W.: If autistic people communicate with spirit beings, how can one explain that they pass on things that are both true and false?

J. Meereboer: Here too I was helped by conversations with Etshevit mediated by Frau Staël von Holstein. Autistic people who can perceive supersensible things experience great spiritual facts primarily because they still live in a pre-birth state in the world of spirit. On the other hand, their expressive capacities are not adequate to convey these mighty spiritual realms in an accurate and differentiated way. It is therefore not that they misperceive something spiritually, but that their power to express it is limited and they are therefore unable to convey everything properly. It may well be that they directly express what they perceive, or their communications with spiritual beings, but that they cannot convey this fully. It can also be the case that such communications do not leave others free. Spiritual visions could for example be expressed in a curtailed and dogmatic way so that they acquire a compulsive character — similar to the way in which autistic people are stuck in a kind of straitjacket in the outer world and the way they relate to it. It may also be that they perceive spiritual tendencies but represent them sometimes in too narrow or dogmatic a way, so that they lose their open-ended nature, conveying nothing of the quality of developing processes. Instead of rhythm one gets rigid bar lines.

Etshevit on autism

W.W.: To conclude, can you say a little of what you have discussed with Etshevit in relation to autism?

J. Meereboer: I've already mentioned previous lives. Among other things I asked whether autistic people tend to incarnate more quickly. Etshevit told me that this varies but that many do indeed incarnate more quickly, and do not get further than the moon sphere after death — in other words do not pass through all the planetary spheres. So they only pass through the kamaloka phase and then return to earth.

Etshevit also said that the nervous system and the brain of autistic people is properly configured but cannot be correctly governed by the I. He spoke of how flow velocity, that is, electric current in the nerves, is probably much quicker than in so-called normal people. I asked him then how the brain is governed in autism if not by the 'I', and he replied that this happens etherically, through etheric currents, and is thus an autonomous dynamic of the etheric body. He also suggested that one could investigate neurotransmitter substances and if one did this one would find that these do not flow properly. Accordingly, etheric and electrical currents flow too fast while messenger substances flow too slowly. These latter are the substances needed to give the brain signals. This means that the astral body is, as it were, 'switched off'. And here Ahriman intervenes, in his attempt to prevent this functioning normally. Ahriman does not want these messenger substances to flow, and this gives autistic people their automatic mode of behaviour. Ahriman would like autistic people to become robotic and not to be able to emerge from this automatism. This is why the higher being, the I, of autistic people wishes to have nothing to do with Ahriman, and why they long for Christ. We should give them human access to Christ.

Etshevit also spoke of how it is a great help to read the Gospel of St John to autistic people. John the Baptist was also a witness — that was his chief work, bearing witness to Christ at the Jordan baptism. Similarly, autistic people are witnesses. They can identify with this role, for during their life they are condemned to be witnesses. They do not develop really, but are only witnesses of what their parents and other people think. They themselves hardly do deeds of any kind. And with the Gospel of St John a kind of religious, supersensible witness-bearing is conveyed, which does autistic people good.

It is very important to remember that autistic people who express themselves with the help of Facilitated Communication have to use concepts that are inadequate for conveying what they perceive, and what they would really like to convey. They have too small a vocabulary for spiritual facts that are too great. Etshevit also confirmed that autistic people cannot distinguish between inner and outer, both in relation to supersensible and sensible realms, and also in the social domain.

I also asked how one might communicate with autistic people without FC, and he replied that we should learn thought transference—in other words develop super-sensible capacities. He also said that we should learn to perceive micro-movements in the physical body—thus movement of eyelids, small grimaces, etc., which we can mostly only perceive in time-lapse films. The feelings of autistic people, he said, were revealed in this body language. More research on this is required.

During conversations with Frau Staël von Holstein about Rudolf Steiner's Curative Education Course, Christian Rosenkreuz was also present as interested spiritual presence. I sometimes therefore also asked what he might have to say on this theme. Channelled by Frau Staël von Holstein he stated that it is very good for us to undertake the Rose Cross meditation when an autistic person is present in the room, and that he will absorb this and experience it. This will help order both his inner and outer world. One has to be experienced and accomplish the meditation in a correct fashion, just as Steiner described it. In other words one builds up very carefully the image of the black cross with the red roses. In this regard Rudolf Steiner also gave a very useful meditation to curative

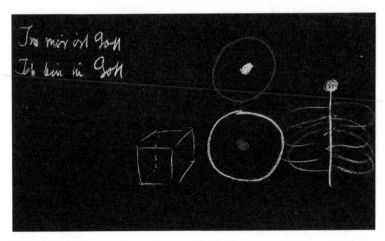

In me is God
I am in God

Rudolf Steiner, board drawing for the Curative Education Course, GA 317. Lecture 10, 5 July 1924

© *Rudolf Steiner Estate Dornach 2011*

teachers, to help them gain insight into the fact that our outer earthly world becomes our inner world between death and a new birth. In the evening one speaks the words 'In me is God', picturing God as the point within the circle; then in the morning one reverses this: 'I am in God' — picturing the I at the centre (see picture). If one meditates on this strongly and correctly in their presence, autistic people are better able to orientate themselves between inner and outer. Christian Rosenkreutz always seeks to help us make anthroposophy more practical if we ask his help.